DOO36923

Dedication

This book is dedicated to recent B.C. historians who are no longer with us, among them Margaret A. Ormsby, Art Downs, R.C. Harris, and Norman Hacking. They served their province well.

Acknowledgements

The author acknowledges with thanks the help he received from Rodger Touchie and Audrey McClellan of Heritage House.

Carving the Western Path

By River, Rail, and Road
Through B.C.'s Southern Mountains

R.G. Harvey

Heritage House
VANCOUVER • VICTORIA • CALGARY

Heritage House Publishing Company Ltd.
#108 – 17665 66A Avenue
Surrey, BC V3S 2A7
www.heritagehouse.ca

Library and Archives Canada Cataloguing in Publication
Harvey, R.G. (Robert Gourlay), 1922-
    Carving the western path: by river, rail, and road through B.C.'s southern
mountains

Includes bibliographical references and index.

ISBN 13: 978-1-895811-62-9
ISBN 10: 1-895811-62-7

1. Railroads—British Columbia—History
2. Roads—British Columbia—History
3. Steam-navigation—British Columbia—History
4. Paddle steamers—British Columbia—History
5. Transportation and state—British Columbia—History
I. Title

HE215.Z7B75 1998   388'.09711   C98-910807-4

Cover and book design: Darlene Nickull
Editor: Audrey McClellan
Printed in Canada

Heritage House acknowledges the financial support for its publishing program
from the Government of Canada through the Book Publishing Industry
Development Program (BPIDP), Canada Council for the Arts, and the British
Columbia Arts Council.

The Canada Council | Le Conseil des Arts
for the Arts | du Canada

BRITISH COLUMBIA
ARTS COUNCIL
Supported by the Province of British Columbia

Contents

Maps

The Asides

Introduction

In *The Coast Connection*, a companion volume to this one, I said that you cannot pour history onto a plate and let it run off haphazardly and still retain the reader's interest.

In *Carving the Western Path* the history is channelled into the story of the fight for transportation supremacy in British Columbia. Roads, rail, and rivercraft vied for routes and government support in different parts of the province, influencing settlement and the success or failure of local commerce.

In the beginning the ocean was the avenue to the northwest coast of North America, and late in the eighteenth century the seagoing adventurers came by sea to a place Captain James Cook had marked as Nutka on his early maps. They traded for the shiny pelts of sea otters with the first inhabitants. Then, with complete confidence in their wind-driven craft, they sailed the Pacific Ocean to China, where furs of this quality were in demand. This enterprise, remarkable as it was, failed to compare with the energy and expertise shown by Captain George Vancouver of the Royal Navy when he charted the inlets, straits, and passages of the unknown coast a few years later.

Meanwhile, 500 miles to the east, men of two competing fur companies were making their first exploratory trips into the Rocky Mountains from the prairies in search of new trade and more furs. First there was Alexander Mackenzie, who missed meeting Vancouver by only a few weeks when he reached the coast in 1793; then Simon Fraser, who stayed; and finally there was the proficient mapmaker David Thompson, who arrived at the mouth of the Columbia just a few weeks too late to offset the Americans' claim of precedence.

The fur brigades constantly hunted new bounty in that wilderness, but rather than carving their own paths through the mountains, these pursuers of the beaver followed the paths already put there by the aboriginal people. The Canadian voyageurs followed the Churchill and Saskatchewan rivers across the continent, then took the Columbia River south of the eventual international boundary to the Pacific at Fort Vancouver, at the division of what are now Washington and Oregon states. The traders preferred this route because of the difficulty of the Fraser Canyon and because of tales told to Simon Fraser of the ferocity of the Native people at the Fraser's mouth. These stories were partially confirmed by the hostility he encountered during his trip there in 1808.

Sea traders disappeared with the depleted sea otter, but the beaver lasted out. The English did not kill off their golden goose; they negotiated it away when Oregon went by treaty to the United States in 1846 and the border was established on the 49th parallel. Out of necessity English fur traders took their chances with the Native people, but they still had to find a way to the coast through or around the Fraser Canyon.

It was gold, not furs, that put the first road for wheeled vehicles into British Columbia. In the middle of the nineteenth century that precious metal was found in the watershed of the Thompson River and then in the sand bars of the Fraser River below the Thompson, causing a huge influx of American and other foreign prospectors, but these finds turned out to be of rather limited duration. It was the discoveries in the Barkerville area, close to the headwaters of the Fraser, that really set up the Colony of British Columbia with a lasting source of revenue located in its interior. This led to the building of the 308-mile Cariboo Road from Yale to Barkerville, begun in 1860 and fully completed in 1866.

This massive project, initiated by James Douglas, the first governor of the colony, rendered the jurisdiction financially paralyzed. Britain graciously handed over this bankrupt western outpost to the new nation of Canada in 1871. While the change of ownership did not include the debentures outstanding for the financing of the road, the new province did inherit the onus and difficulty of maintaining 308 miles of road in undeveloped and mostly mountainous terrain.

One indication of how meagre the resources of the Colony of Vancouver Island were after the gold miners left came to light when Governor Arthur Edward Kennedy arrived from Western Australia in March 1864 after Governor Douglas's retirement. His new outpost of the British Empire was in precarious financial condition, dependent mainly on the gold of its mainland neighbour. Mindful of activities in his previous domain, Kennedy proposed what became known as "The Vancouver Island Exploratory Expedition of 1864," presumably to unlock the hidden treasures north of Victoria. He offered to match every dollar contributed by the public with up to two dollars from the public purse. The expedition led to a modest gold find at Leechtown near Victoria and confirmed the coal at Nanaimo, but it did little else. Very soon the British government combined the two colonies, answering the wishes of the Vancouver Islanders. The mainlanders of the original British Columbia found themselves irreversibly tied to a penniless offshore partner.[1]

After the enlarged British Columbia joined confederation, a continent-wide economic depression in the 1870s assured continuing money shortages. It was many years before the province built any more long-distance trunk roads.

The dearth of roadbuilding extended to one area where a through road was most necessary: the lower valley of the Fraser River from New Westminster to Yale. More settlers were arriving in the valley and beginning to develop the huge agricultural potential of the area, and a road would have supplemented the movement of freight via rivercraft to and from the Cariboo Road, which terminated at Yale. Wagon trains were outpaced by the sternwheelers, but they could carry a steady volume more

Governor James Douglas suffered from his dour appearance. The ends of his mouth seemed permanently turned down. But the Celtic/Hispanic racial mix often produces remarkable results and he was no exception: his father was a Scotsman and his mother of noble Creole stock. Douglas had nothing but contempt for the itinerant miners who burst upon him in 1858, seeking wealth without work, but he strove for their interests as he realised that was best for the colony. He could not abide the aristocratic English immigrants, but he forged a good working partnership with Colonel Richard Moody of the Royal Engineers to produce their joint masterpiece, the Cariboo Road. In his handling of the finances of the young colonies he was nothing less than a genius. In other words, he was a great man.

consistenetly, and with better economy on a year round basis. The government attempted to build a permanent road from New Westminster, but expensive measures were needed to counter disastrous spring floods that occurred on the Fraser in these years, and the new jurisdiction simply did not have the resources.

And what of the rest of British Columbia? The trails that there were, mainly created by Native people or the fur brigades, were best described by Lieutenant Henry Palmer of the Royal Engineers, who wrote in 1862:

> It is difficult to find language to express in adequate terms the utter vileness of the trails…dreaded alike by all classes of travellers…slippery precipitous ascents and descents, fallen logs, overhanging branches, roots, rocks, turbid pools, and miles of deep mud.[2]

For much of the slowly growing non-Native population in the 1870s and 1880s, there was a constant and compelling need to travel. Many were nomads on a constant quest for the end of the rainbow. Those who had preceded the seekers of gold, particularly the members of the coastal aboriginal nations, were immune to it, as were the men and women inhabiting the remote and well-separated cattle ranches in the grasslands of the Cariboo or the Thompson, Okanagan, or Nicola areas, but they were small in number compared to the swirling population of gold-hungry adventurers who were still rushing to the sporadic finds of placer gold—discoveries that all, unfortunately, proved to be limited.

There was little permanent settlement in the Interior, and with the exception of the Cariboo Road there were no roads, especially over the mountains east of Yale, towards today's Okanagan and Kootenay regions. There, travellers relied on the canoe, and after that, in tune with the development of the steam engine, sternwheelers moved onto the rivers and lakes. The British Columbia's Interior had a wonderful supply of them and in the absence of roads, the sternwheelers thrived.

These graceful craft dominated movement in British Columbia's southern Interior and the Fraser Valley prior to the arrival of the transcontinental railway and, in some places, after it. They moved people very comfortably as they searched for gold or a place to settle; they moved goods, mostly from mine to smelter or farm to market; and they did it all at a pace and in a manner suitable to the times. There were at one time over 300 sternwheelers active on B.C.'s waters. Most were plying the lower Fraser River or Okanagan, Kootenay, or Arrow Lakes. Others, less in number, were scattered throughout the central and northern Interior, all following the quest for gold.

The problems came when the times changed and the sternwheelers gave way to road or rail. This did not happen overnight—it took a few years—but when they departed they left a great number of settlements (and in some places quite large towns) by the water's edge. These had been reached easily by the paddlewheel but were difficult to access by road.

When the railways entered the picture they caused an even bigger problem by blocking out the possible routes for roads and discouraging competition from roadbuilders. In light of this statement, consider the following.

British Columbia abounds with mountains. In the southern half of the province their alignment is a challenge to the movement of goods and people eastwards or westwards. "Easy" passes through these ranges are few and far between. Consider that the first railway into the province seized hold of the most vital of all these openings, the Fraser Canyon, and not only occupied it but destroyed the remarkable Cariboo Wagon Road that had been built only fifteen years earlier. Consider also that the same railway at the same time took over the only usable pass through the Selkirk Mountains, Rogers Pass, and held that for its own exclusive use.

These expropriations by Canada's first national railway—and that is what they were—denied the people of British Columbia the use of the Fraser Canyon for a roadway for 40 years and the use of Rogers Pass for the same purpose for twice that long.

Then there was Eagle Pass, probably one of the lowest and most easily approached ways through some of B.C.'s steepest mountains, the Monashee Range. There a road appeared with the railway, then mysteriously disappeared, repeating this process several times over a span of more than twenty years, depriving British Columbians of a continuous road link between the Columbia and Fraser watersheds for this period.

The same railway company, this time operating under another name, interfered with the road authority's use of Allison Pass through the Cascade Mountains at the end of the first decade of this century, a time so pivotal that a road was not built through it until the end of the fifth decade.

Notwithstanding all of the above, I do not deny that the Canadian Pacific Railway was a wonderful boost to British Columbia after it began its life as a province of Canada. The CPR brought contact with the rest of the nation; it brought immigrants; it brought trade; eventually it brought the interchange of goods with the other Pacific Rim countries; it started the export of B.C.'s resources in a big way. Unfortunately it also brought the destruction or abandonment of the few and far between wagon roads through the mountains. And once these roads were destroyed or abandoned, the railroad pressured governments in both Ottawa and Victoria to discourage the development of other modes of transportation (primarily the building of roads alongside the railway tracks).

Trains were of course much more comfortable than a dusty or mud-beset stagecoach, but the stagecoach had many more opportunities to divert and take more people to more points. After the arrival of the railroad, once a traveller left the "iron road," he or she often found fewer means of reaching more distant points— and fewer roadhouses en route. The hardy and independent pioneers also resented being dependent on one carrier, especially when the CPR bought up all the rail opposition and the lake and river craft in the Kootenays, or when it fell into the excesses of monopoly in terms of freight rates and fare prices.

An argument can be made against building the Canadian Northern Railway (now part of the Canadian National Railway), mainly on the basis of its timing, but not against the creation of the CPR.

In the case of the sternwheelers, no one can speak rationally against their suitability to provide the mobility the pioneers needed early on or their magnificence in their final form. However, they were limited by their inability to move when the lakes and rivers were fully frozen, which happened more often then than now, as well as by their vulnerability to low water, log jams, and sudden floods, their slow speed, and their habit of creating communities peculiarly difficult to serve by other means.

The road authority had its problems with the railway mo-nopolies and settlement patterns established by the sternwheelers, yet roads were eventually built in all areas of the province.

This story commences in southern B.C., the focus of this volume. Section One covers the riverboat era on the lower Fraser, pursuing the theme of river, rail, and road through the mountains across southern B.C. from New Westminster to Kamloops and on to Revelstoke and Golden. This has long been the most important transportation corridor in the province. The transportation channel from Crowsnest Pass along the American border to Hope is the subject of Section Two. A second volume will document a similar corridor across the province from Yellowhead Pass to the mouth of the Skeena River and will look at the province north of the Skeena. Together the two volumes recount the building of highways and railways in four separate areas, each deeply affected by the era of the sternwheelers. As in *The Coast Connection* there are numerous boxed anecdotes and explanatory features and many maps.

R.G. Harvey,
Victoria, B.C.

This book deals greatly with banks for rivers. In some parts of the world they treat rivers very much like ships. If you are at the centre of a river and facing downstream, the bank on your right is the right bank and the one on your left, the left. The author uses this convention and the reader is hereby warned of this.

Customary to the times when these events occurred, distances and other measures are given in miles and feet rather than in metric measure.

All maps are the work of the author.

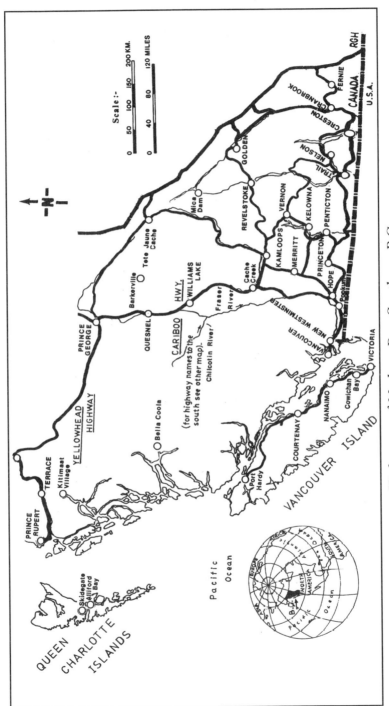

Highways of Modern-Day Southern B.C.

Section One

The Lower Fraser River and Its Canyon, the Thompson and the South Thompson Rivers and Their Valleys, and Eagle, Rogers, and Kicking Horse Passes

Chapter 1

The Fraser River and Its Lower Valley

Everything goes upstream to the one and only wagon road, and nothing comes back—except the gold!

The first steamboat on the Fraser River was the Hudson's Bay Company's (HBC) original, the SS *Beaver*, a side paddlewheeler. For many years after it appeared in 1836 it was used for supplying naval vessels. Then it was used by the British Admiralty for surveying coastal waters (as the HMS *Beaver* with a swivel gun up front) and to transport important individuals of the HBC, primarily Chief Factor James Douglas. It was never used as a long-haul cargo vessel because it had to load such a massive amount of cordwood to steam any distance at all that it could carry very little else. It carried up to fifteen woodcutters when on a long trip requiring its best possible speed, and on such a trip it would consume up to nine cords of wood a day.[1]

The coalfields at both Fort Rupert (near present-day Port McNeill at the northern tip of Vancouver Island) and Nanaimo eventually provided more compact fuel, and the Beaver's efficiency

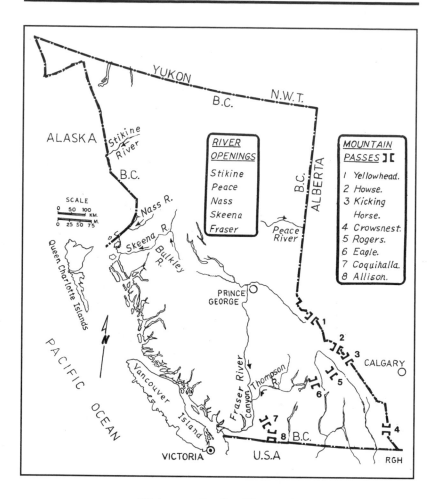

Thirteen Paths Through
British Columbia's Mountains

There are two ways to travel through a mountain range, either by a pass or along a river's course. Over time, travellers have entered B.C. from the east and from the ocean using eight passes and five rivers.

Yellowhead Pass. First called Leather Pass by the Northwesters for the hides they took through to New Caledonia, it was later named for an Iroquois halfbreed trapper. The elevation is 1131 metres (3711 feet). It joins the Fraser and the Mackenzie watersheds, crossing the Park Ranges of the Rocky Mountains.

Howse Pass. A pass of aboriginal use, it was identified and used by David Thompson of the North West Company in 1807, but named for Joseph Howse of the Hudson's Bay Company who first used it three years later. The elevation is 1524 metres (5000 feet). It joins the Columbia and the North Saskatchewan River watersheds.

Kicking Horse Pass. *First named by Dr. (later Sir) James Hector of the Palliser Expedition in 1859. The elevation is 1622 metres (5322 feet). It joins the Columbia and the South Saskatchewan River watersheds. Both it and Howse Pass go through the Continental Ranges of the Rocky Mountains.*

Crowsnest Pass. *First indicated by the Palliser Expedition in its map of 1859, though that group did not visit the pass. It is 1357 metres (4452 feet) in height and joins the Columbia and the South Saskatchewan watersheds. It crosses the Border Ranges of the Rocky Mountains.*

Rogers Pass. *Named after A.B. Rogers, and discovered either in 1881 or, based on one claim, 1866. The elevation of the pass is 1323 metres (4340 feet). The pass is totally within the Columbia River watershed. It passes across the main upper spine of the Selkirk Range of the Columbia Mountains, joining both ends of the big bend of the Columbia River.*

Eagle Pass. *Discovered by Walter Moberly in 1865. The elevation of the pass is 561 metres (1841 feet). The pass connects the Fraser and Columbia watersheds, crossing a mountain range originally called the Gold Range and now named the Monashee Range of the Columbia Mountains. (In the early days the Selkirks included the Monashee and the Purcell Ranges.)*

Coquihalla Pass. *Native peoples originally used this pass, and in 1872 the first white settlers of the south-central Interior used it as a cattle trail. The elevation is 1674 metres (5492 feet) and it is totally within the Fraser watershed. It crosses the Hozameen Range of the Cascade Mountains.*

Allison Pass. *Named after John Fall Allison, it was discovered by him in 1860. The elevation of the pass is 1352 metres (4436 feet). The pass, along with the Sumallo Summit, connects the Fraser and Columbia watersheds. It passes through the Hozameen Range of the Cascade Mountains.*

River Openings. *The Stikine, Nass, and Skeena/Bulkley river systems flow through the Coast Mountains to the Pacific Ocean. The Fraser, its canyon the divider between the Coast and the Cascade Mountains, does the same. The Peace River flows straight through the Rocky Mountains.*

(Note: This listing and the map feature only those locations mentioned in the text. Ground elevations shown are above sea level and are taken from The Atlas of British Columbia.*)*

The Beaver *merited its captain's description: "as sturdy a craft for her size as was ever put afloat." Those who examined the oak and greenheart timbers of huge dimension agreed with this. After a maiden voyage in the English Channel, the master reported, "Should the engines go wrong, she will answer as a sailing vessel perfectly well," and that was how the* Beaver *went around Cape Horn, out to Hawaii, and finally to British Columbia, arriving at the mouth of the Fraser on April 10, 1836. Sad indeed that after grounding in First Narrows of Burrard Inlet in July 1888 the boat was never refloated, or at least dismantled and reassembled in a museum. Its sturdiness prevented this—how do you dismantle something made of 10" by 10" oak timbers while it is balanced on a rock surrounded by one of the strongest tidal currents anywhere? Nature only could do that, and did so within five years.*

was much improved. By that time it had been joined by the *Labouchere* and the *Otter* (propeller driven and of deeper draft). The *Beaver* and the *Otter* featured prominently in James Douglas's inauguration as the first governor of the Colony of British Columbia, carrying the official party to Fort Langley in November 1858.[2] The *Otter* distinguished itself by carrying $200,000 in gold, including a single nugget of over 46 ounces from Dease, picked up at the mouth of the Stikine and brought to Victoria in 1874.

Previous to that, in early July 1858, the first American steamboat, appropriately named the *Surprise*, nosed into Fort

Langley landing, seeking a pilot to guide it to Hope, drawn by the word of gold. A month later the *Umatilla*, another Yankee, made it as far as Yale, and it was shortly joined on the Fraser by the *Enterprise*, a boat under Captain William Irving. His son (Captain John Irving) and Captain William Moore were to dominate the steamboat business in the years following, when the complement of steamboats operating on the Fraser River more than doubled.[3]

Captain Irving, senior, lost little time in entering British Columbia's folklore. He was libelled, in his opinion, in a pamphlet called *The Scorpion* that was printed by the *Columbian* newspaper in New Westminster. "If they insult me they stay on dry land!" was probably his response—or words to that effect but unprintable. His retribution was to refuse to carry the *Columbian* on his boats from then on. When public outrage rose, he answered it by extending his ban to all newspapers unless a surcharge of $50 a copy was paid. This confrontation was with a newspaper whose editor, John Robson, was to become the premier of the province before many years passed. Counteraction by the newspaper is hard to detect because the news media berated almost everyone in those days. Robson denied having anything to do with the article, but Irving refused to believe him. Bruce Hutchinson, in his report on this, adds, "Soon the *Scorpion* ceased to sting and later expired."[4]

These two resolute mariners, Irving and Moore, came to B.C. from service on the lower Columbia River, and as far as is known the vessels mentioned came from that area or from San Francisco where they were built—the Seattle area boatbuilding industry was yet to emerge. To reach the Fraser River they had to brave the outer coastal waters. That took courage and determination, which they had in good measure. The lower Fraser River's romance with the paddlewheeler was under way, and there were good men to start it off. Although most were Americans, Governor Douglas insisted that they fly the Union Jack.

When the economy of the West Coast plunged in the early 1870s, Irving and his competitors faced up to it in a rather

The original Enterprise *was the second sternwheeler to arrive on the Fraser River in 1858. This boat was profitable for the owners, making $25,000 for one trip to Murderer's Bar. It outlasted a host of early gold-rush steamers, many of which stayed only one summer. Details of its demise are not known, but one supposition is that its engine and boiler were packed in from Port Douglas to Soda Creek to be used in the second* Enterprise, *launched at Alexandria in the Cariboo in 1863.*

Captain William Irving (left) was a successful sternwheeler skipper and maritime entrepreneur, scornful of criticism by the printed word. Irving handed down his enterprise and energy to his son John (right). Captain John Irving started an outstanding career in British Columbia's river, lake, and coastal waters shipping industry when he became a company president while still in his teens after the death of his father.

Captain William Moore's (centre) arrival on the West Coast predated the existence of British Columbia. He came to Vancouver Island from Hanover, Germany, via the U.S.A., picking up American citizenship on the way. He was involved in the short-lived Queen Charlotte Islands gold rush in 1852. While his base, until his death in 1909, was in Victoria, he was in on every gold rush there was, building and losing sternwheelers frequently, with numerous bankruptcies.

remarkable way—they alternated year about on the route. William Irving died in 1872 and was succeeded by his son John, who became an entrepreneur of note (as well as pioneering the Fraser River, he was also a driving force in the Columbia & Kootenay Steam Navigation Company, the company that brought the sternwheeler in its full glory to the southern Interior), an ingenious negotiator, and a prominent figure in B.C.'s maritime history.

Moore was more restless and followed the scent of gold everywhere. He went bankrupt a total of seven times in his business career. Every time he had money he would build another sternwheeler or, if he didn't have enough, a sailing schooner or even a barge or two. He saw a gold rush as a transportation opportunity. In B.C. in those days it was a risky business but a wonderful one.

To shift forward in time, the last sternwheeler on the river was the *Skeena*, which was built in Vancouver for Burns & Co. to distribute meat to the builders of the Grand Trunk Pacific Railway on the river of its name, then returned to southern waters and finally tied up at New Westminster in 1925.[5] In between these beginnings and endings the river saw many craft, and most were eminently successful. Of the exceptions, the *Royal City* burned at Mission in April 1901, killing two people, while the *Ramona* blew up near Fort Langley a week later and four people died. William West built the *Royal City* at Fort Langley. He used an engine and boiler that he got for a low price in Seattle because there was trouble with the steam pressure regulator. His father repaired that part, but obviously it did not stay fixed for very long.[6]

Another very popular paddlewheeler in these years was the *Yosemite*. It started its career south of the border and was carrying passengers on the Sacramento River in October 1865 when it blew its boilers and killed 55 persons. Repaired and put on the market, it was purchased by John Irving and gave wonderful service without further misbehaviour for many years, although it was viewed with considerable foreboding when it first arrived.[7] Many more of the estimated 300 paddlewheelers in B.C. came to an

The last sternwheeler in action on the Fraser River in B.C., the Skeena *survived its sister ships' steady demise until it also went to the scrapheap after the death of its owner in 1925.*

The Yosemite *had two paddlewheels, one each side, which were 32 feet in diameter and 10 feet wide. It made a heavy wake and legend has it that it was the* Yosemite's *waves that swept the* Beaver *into the depths of First Narrows in 1893.*

inglorious end in one way or another, but all in all they were a wonderful means of transport in their half century.

One of the inglorious incidents might well have influenced the course of B.C.'s transportation history. It involved one of the first sternwheelers built in British Columbia, a vessel named the *Fort Yale*, which left Hope for Yale on a Sunday afternoon, April 14, 1861. As was customary, Captain Smith Jamieson entertained guests in his wheelhouse until the dinner gong sounded. These passengers were just sitting down in the dining room when the boiler blew up right under the wheelhouse, which took leave of the boat and floated off down the river. Captain Jamieson disappeared with it and his remains were not found for some time.[8]

Two other crew members died, as well as one unfortunate guest who had stayed on in the wheelhouse. The lucky ones who were unhurt included William Irving, important as the progenitor of John, and George Landvoigt, who later became the road superintendent at Hope. At the time of his lucky escape, Landvoigt was working with Thomas Spence on his bridge, where the town of that name now lies, and subsequently he became an accomplished trailbuilder out of Hope. Jamieson was one of five brothers who all died in steamboat mishaps, four of them explosions. Bruce Hutchinson, the newspaperman who gave us the story of Captain Irving in his book *The Fraser*, also tells us that Captain Jamieson was hastening to return to New Westminster to marry an American actress. He probably had the steam pressure regulator tied down as they often did.[9] (The steam regulator was a safety valve that opened when steam pressure in the boiler reached a certain level. If the pressure was allowed to rise unchecked as the crew threw more and more wood into the fire—and more pressure meant more speed—it ultimately split open the tubes in the boiler, which promptly blew it up.)

The sternwheelers could proceed only as far as Yale on the Fraser River. Black Canyon and Hells Gate Canyon, immediately upstream of Yale, were impossible to navigate. The only vessel to achieve the impossible was the *Skuzzy*, built with twenty watertight

Andrew Onderdonk launched the Skuzzy *on May 4, 1882. He hired Captains S.R. and David Smith, brothers—the first-mentioned the only man to take a steamer down the Snake River—and they lined the* Skuzzy *through the Black Canyon to Hells Gate to serve the construction crews and defy Premier Walkem's $10-per-ton levy on freight on the Cariboo Road. This feat required the full power of the engines plus the pulling power of 125 Chinese labourers. The boat had twenty watertight bulkheads and steamed through Hells Gate Canyon before being dismantled. Its parts were used to build the* Skuzzy II, *which Onderdonk used on the Thompson River to finish the railway construction in that area.*

compartments and winched and dragged through both canyons using its own winches and the power of 125 Chinese labourers. It was built by railway contractor Andrew Onderdonk in 1882.

From Yale travellers embarked on the Cariboo Road, which ran from Yale to Barkerville and on to Camerontown, a distance of about 380 miles. It was 18 to 22 feet wide, with a surface of broken stone as far as it followed the Fraser and Thompson valleys, with lesser gravel thereafter. One old-timer reported, "No mud between Yale and Spences Bridge. Nothing to make mud." This road was built under the direction of Her Majesty Queen Victoria's Corps of Royal Engineers, Colonel Richard C. Moody commanding. The Royal Engineers physically built it most of the

This shows the ominous entrance to the southern Fraser Canyon just upstream of Yale, B.C., the end of Lower Fraser navigation.

way between Yale and Spuzzum, and with the help of contractors thereafter.

Construction of the road commenced in 1860 and was generally complete by 1866. It was a toll road and contained two toll bridges, the Alexandra Bridge near Spuzzum, and Spence's Bridge over the Thompson where the town of Spences Bridge now lies. Between these structures the road was built by the bridge builders. Joseph Trutch completed the 17 miles from Spuzzum to Boston Bar, and Thomas Spence the 26 miles from Boston Bar to Lytton (today's mileages), the work supervised by his foreman George Landvoigt. From that point to Spences Bridge, 23 miles, others took over, and finally Gustavus Blin Wright built right through to Soda Creek, 280 miles from Yale. Wagons moved singly from Yale to Boston Bar, as that stretch was of lesser width. At Boston Bar they formed up into longer mule or oxen trains pulling double wagons. The road was a success from the day of its completion, with express stagecoaches reaching the water transport at Soda Creek in a record time of 30 hours. Wright went on with the work from Soda Creek through Quesnel to Cottonwood, 20 miles from Barkerville, and a man named Munro completed it to that point in 1866. A connection from Cache Creek to Savona's Ferry, at the bottom end of Kamloops Lake, was also built. The extremely difficult thirteen miles from Yale to Spuzzum was built by the Royal Engineers. It is a distance of eleven miles today.[10]

At Boston Bar, shown here, wagons were doubled up with two or three times as many oxen, as seen in the distance, heading towards Barkerville. To this point on the short trip from Yale, two oxen pulled single wagons as the road was so narrow and winding.

The Fraser River boats could also move through to Harrison Lake, thanks to the Royal Engineers who dredged the Harrison River in 1859 and 1860. They did this very ingeniously by installing rock dykes and piling to confine the river's flow and thereby create a deeper channel.[11] This was part of Governor James Douglas's first effort to get the gold miners further up the Fraser River. In 1860 Douglas made a notable trip to Lillooet, first going to Port Douglas by sternwheeler. Then a 38-mile hike and 5 miles in a rowboat took him to Lillooet Lake, where he was met by a small steamboat that took him to Port Pemberton. Back on land he negotiated the 30-mile trail to Anderson Lake and travelled the length of it on the *Lady of the Lake*. Finally he walked the short portage to Seton Lake, where plied the *Champion*. He must have arrived foot weary and seat weary![12]

This trip probably helped Douglas decide to build a road through the Fraser Canyon, a more direct route than the Port Douglas to Lillooet trail. In 1897 the Port Douglas-Lillooet Road was rebuilt after 36 years of neglect, presumably beside the remains of various steamboats. This was probably simply a pathetic attempt by the provincial government to salve its conscience for allowing the CPR to destroy the Fraser Canyon portion of the Cariboo Road. Mostly due to its own short-sightedness, the road authority expended much labour and many dollars of the taxpayers' money in a futile attempt to make this circuitous route a feasible alternative. Instead, Port Douglas met its inevitable demise and the route fell back into disuse.[13]

Although the building of the CPR was detrimental to the wagon roads, it gave a tremendous boost to the sternwheeler transportation business. That eloquent traveller Newton Chittenden describes a trip in August 1882 from Victoria to Yale on the best of them, the *R.P. Rithet*, which made its maiden voyage that year with Captain John Irving at the helm. Chittenden, an American from Connecticut, survived the Civil War with the rank of captain and travelled extensively in North America, coming to British Columbia in 1882. He published his *Travels in British*

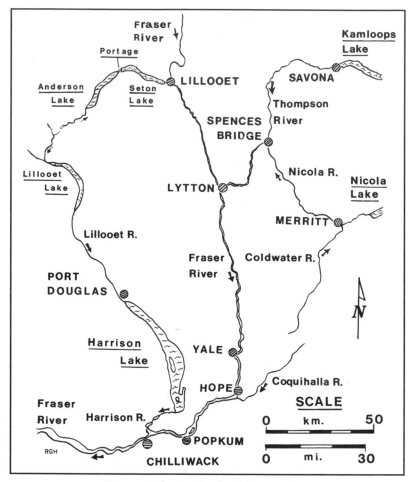

Rivers Through the Mountains

This shows various rivers that provided ways through the mountains in the early days. From the left:

1. *By the Harrison River and its lake, then the Lillooet River and its lake, then by the lake chain to Lillooet. Governor Douglas had over a hundred would-be gold miners build a trail between the lakes in 1858, but it was never really used after that.*

2. *By the Fraser River through its canyon from Hope to Lytton, then north by the Thompson and a route north off from it and east by Kamloops Lake. This was the Cariboo Road route with its connection to Savona, built between 1860 and 1866 and used ever after.*

3. *A trail was built between 1872 and 1876 from Hope by the Coquihalla and Coldwater Rivers to Merritt and on north. It was demolished in great part by the railway that opened for business on this route in 1916, but it was restored in great glory as a highway in 1986.*

Columbia the same year. He was ecstatic about the potential of the province and the building of the CPR, which he reports on at length. In his Introduction he wrote, "There is probably no portion of the North American Continent, within the confines of government and civilisation, concerning which the general public has less definite and reliable information, than British Columbia." Chittenden set out to put that right.

The *Rithet*, named after Irving's partner, was the first vessel on the coast to employ hydraulics to assist the steering. It was 200 feet in length, 39 feet wide, 686 tons, and was equipped with large and elegant staterooms and other facilities to accommodate 250 passengers, moving them at a speed of 13 knots. It was fully equal to the *Bonnington* and its sister ships in the Interior, and besides transporting supplies to the railway builders it also assisted greatly with the population and sustenance of the Gulf Islands, along with the *William Irving* and the *Reliance*. These riverboats did not hesitate to cross the Strait of Georgia. Captain Moore continued to provide competition to Irving, first with his *Henrietta*, then with his fine boat the *Western Slope*.[14]

It is not right to leave the story of the early steamboats on the Lower Fraser without at least one example of the humour that was never far from the surface. A case in point was the *Union*, which was always known as the SS *Sudden Jerk*. This boat was in fact a barge powered by a steam engine from a thresher, taken from a farmer's field, and it had some drawbacks. There was no reverse gear, so to effect an emergency stop the captain had to throw a roll of sacking into the gears. As well, the engine could not assume a load gradually; to start a tow the *Sudden Jerk*'s captain had to leave some slack in the towline and take a run at it, hence the name.[15]

One reason for the paddlewheelers' success was the lack of any dependable alternative means of transport up the Fraser Valley, a situation which changed radically when the Canadian Pacific Railway started service along the north bank of the river from New Westminster to Yale in 1886. Even after that, many of the

S.S. Rithet

S.S. William Irving

The Rithet, *the* William Irving, *the* Reliance, *and the* Western Slope— *four good ships on the lower Fraser in the 1880s. The last-mentioned belonged to Captain William Moore, and it triggered competition from the other three, which were owned by Captain John Irving. These vessels, and others like them, carried freight for the Cariboo Road wagons for many years, then contributed wonderfully to the railway construction along the north side of the Fraser from Pitt River to Yale. The* William Irving, *when loaded with 300 tons of freight, drew three feet of water. All these boats operated profitably for many years.*

S.S. Reliance

S.S. Western Slope

rivercraft stayed in operation and this gracious way of moving people and freight endured for another quarter of a century because there was still the south bank of the Fraser River to be served. It was the completion of the B.C. Electric Railway from Vancouver to Chilliwack in 1910 that spelled the end, an event hastened on by the opening of the Canadian Northern Pacific Railway a few years later.[16]

The poor condition of the road on the south side of the Fraser River certainly contributed to the sternwheelers' longevity. Robert

Beaven was both the premier and the Chief Commissioner of Lands and Works for British Columbia for the years 1872 through 1876, and again in 1882. After the provincial assembly approved the construction of what became known as the Old Yale Road from Ladner to Yale in 1874, he strove to fulfill its wishes, and he thought for a while that he had done so, but the river had other ideas.

George Landvoigt, by this time the road superintendent at Hope, reported in both 1876 and 1877 that the first 25 miles of the road west of town were impassable for months on end. In 1876 this was due to freshet damage and in 1877 he mentions other causes such as a bridge being destroyed by the wild cattle driven over it. In later years the cattle were shipped by sternwheeler when the beef industry could afford it. (During this period, roadbuilding along the northern side of the river was decisively discouraged when 27 acres of the riverbank slid into the water at

As Chief Commissioner of Lands and Works from 1872 to 1876, the Honourable Robert Beaven tried to build a lasting road from Chilliwack to Hope, the most unstable part of the through road on the south side of the Fraser to Ladner. Bad spring floods in the springs of 1875 and 1876 frustrated him and the road was never permanent for a number of miles south of Hope until the turn of the century. Beaven served again in the Lands and Works portfolio in 1882-3 when he was also premier. In a speech to the Legislature he forecast a wagon road from Hope over Coquihalla Pass to the interior, but British Columbia had to wait for 110 years for his prophecy to come true.

During the Chilliwack Flood of 1894, boats and rafts were the order of the day for all residents of Chilliwack. This was the worst spring freshet river flood of all time in British Columbia. Floods in 1876 and in 1948 came close but did not equal it. It affected the Fraser and the Columbia watersheds with equal severity.

Haney. This happened on February 28, 1880.) It was of course the availability of riverboat service that led the Department of Public Works to spend its roadbuilding dollars elsewhere in these years, rather than on a road they had little chance to save in any case.[17] According to department records it was not until 1891 that the section of the Old Yale Road from Chilliwack to Hope could be considered in any way permanent.

The worst flood-prone sections of that pioneer roadway were located upstream of the small settlement of Popkum, a hamlet about 30 kilometres west of Hope. Above Popkum, the river in times of freshet changed course frequently, sometimes scouring as far in as the rock bluffs, and when that happened the road simply disappeared. Downstream of that point the channel moved away from the southern mountains, the Skagit Range of the Cascades, and left the road alone.

Martin Stevens Starret, who was born in Hope in 1888 and was interviewed for the B.C. Archives' Aural History Program in 1963, remembers the sternwheelers calling in regularly in his childhood. His father was a successor to George Landvoigt in looking after the roads and trails. The riverboats could not function when drift ice was in the river, and Starret recalls that at these times the mailman would use a shovel-nosed cedar dugout canoe, never going overland. The shovel-nosed canoe was also their ferry across the Fraser. Starret says, "The main idea in travelling through this thickly flowing chunk-ice is to dodge the big ones, run over the smaller ones, use your head continually and keep cool."

He recalls that the Collins Overland Telegraph Line ran through Hope originally, but they lost it when the CPR came in and the telegraph connection and their post office went across the river. As a result, when the road went out in flood they were completely cut off until the waters went down sufficiently to let the boats operate. Ferry service was late in coming and was sporadic and unreliable when it was in place. Starret confirms that the first sternwheeler tied up at Hope in 1858.[18]

A footnote to the mention of the Collins Telegraph is reported by Corday Mackay, historian and librarian at Vancouver's Lord Byng High School. When the telegraph reached Hope, the first message sent to New Westminster was signed "Landvoigt." It was sent on August 18, 1865, and it was addressed to the Colonial Hotel, instructing them to send a bottle of champagne up to the room of Captain Conway of the Collins company. A nice touch by the road superintendent at Hope. It is a remarkable coincidence that two men who stood out in B.C.'s early transportation history—George Landvoigt and William Moore—both came from Hanover, Germany.[19]

Chapter 2

Hope to Kamloops

The Canadian Pacific Railway builds through the Fraser/Thompson gateway and it's over and out for the Royal Engineers' road

They say that it was created when a huge lake of meltwater from the last ice sheet burst through its barrier of ice and shattered the folded granite of the mountains as it rushed out to the sea, an event geologists believe occurred 11,000 years ago.[1] But the imported Chinese labourers and the beleaguered English-speaking adventurers who made up the majority of the crew that built a railway there over a hundred years ago were convinced that the Fraser Canyon was made by the devil. They cursed Lucifer steadily as they laboured and suffered, fell to their deaths, or blew themselves up. Their travail and agony started in the year 1880.

Young Andrew Onderdonk, in charge of it all although he was barely 30 years old, also felt the demon's breath. The satanic curse of the place stayed with him for four years until he came out the other end at Lytton with his creditors hounding him and with multiple deaths and injuries in his work force of 7000 men behind him.[2] The aristocratic and efficient American contractor, supported by San Francisco money, spent one night in jail at the instigation of his suppliers, but he completed one of the most difficult railway projects in hard rock ever attempted, with 27 short but difficult tunnels in 60 miles.[3] After this he speeded up and cut corners from Lytton to Savona, reaching that point in the fall of 1884.

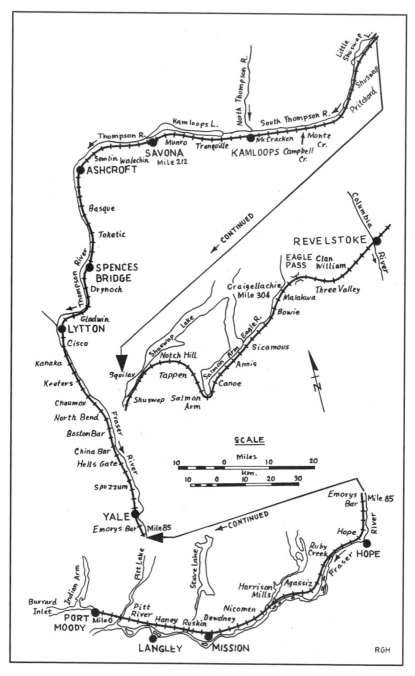

*The Canadian Pacific Railway
from Port Moody to Revelstoke*

Calling for bids on a project like the CPR rail line construction from Emory to Savona was certainly enough to give the dominion government pause for thought. This was the late 1870s, after all, and the area was at the end of civilization, at the other side of the continent. The closest, largest, and most easily accessible centre with the required resources for such a project was San Francisco. It is little wonder that the contractor that got the job, a syndicate led by Andrew Onderdonk, was from there.

Going fully into the intricacies of the tendering process and financing of the CPR is out of place here, but briefly, the core of the B.C. section was to be built by the dominion government and then given to the railway company, which would guarantee that it would maintain and run the track efficiently. The Yale to Kamloops section was to be complete by or before 1885, while Port Moody to Yale was to be done by or before 1891. Onderdonk started off working on contracts for the Canadian government. Later, when he was building from Savona east, his contracts were handed over to the CPR by the government.

For building the railway across the whole country, the CPR was initially given a $24 million subsidy and a 25-million-acre land grant. This was subsequently changed and made much larger to help the CPR finance the construction and start-up of the railway. First the company issued bonds, using the land grant as security, but large-scale land sale was not possible without settlers, and settlement would only follow the completion of the railway— a chicken-and-egg situation. The bonds did not sell so the CPR issued stock with a guaranteed 3 percent interest on the shares, but there was a downturn in the market and the stocks did not sell. Finally the company directors went hat in hand to the government for a $25 million loan, promising to finish the railroad

This map shows Andrew Onderdonk and Michael Haney's remarkable feat of building a railway over terrain between Yale and Ashcroft where engineering difficulties were not exceeded anywhere in the world. They built 304 miles in less than five years in a land that had absolutely nothing in the way of railway or mechanical engineering experience or resources.

17 Mile Post (Cariboo Road) and Fraser River. This was the road alongside which Andrew Onderdonk had to build a railway and at the same time keep the traffic moving. A close look shows a horse and buggy crossing a wooden structure, the outside legs of which are longer than the inside, hence the term, "grasshopper trestle."

Andrew Onderdonk (right), the aristocratic American railway building contractor.

Michael Haney (left) was known as Big Mike or the Irish Prince when he contracted for the CPR. Unfortunately, historians consistently have substituted a second "e" instead of an "a" in his last name when reporting on the builder of the White Pass and Yukon Railway. Michael J. Haney never got credit for what Michael J. Heney did at Skagway. This is one of the regrettable results of historians slavishly quoting their antecedents—mistakes in spelling are carried forward.

five years earlier. They got $22.5 million in the midst of great political turmoil. As the government was now holding a mortgage on the railway, the CPR could not sell shares, so these were promptly converted back into bonds. The government took the equivalent of its loan in bonds, bought another $5 million worth of them, and the CPR put $15 million worth of bonds up for sale, guaranteed by the government, and that is how it built the railway. (When the Grand Trunk Pacific and the Canadian Northern were looking for financing, the settlers were already available because of the CPR, so the GTP and CN's attempt to sell land to raise money for trackage worked better. These two companies also had their bonds, and in some cases the interest, guaranteed by the government. When the railroads' viability came into question, the government was forced to foreclose in both cases and create the government-owned Canadian National Railway. Thus Canada built its national railways!)

In the case of the CPR, there was a process of bidding at the outset, ostensibly to decide who was to get the work, but mostly for appearance's sake. For this the Yale to Port Moody section was split into four sections. If you tendered on a railway contract in 1880 and were not successful, you could buy the contract, but then you had to do the work at the lower price. It is said that Onderdonk paid out $225,000 to buy the first contracts from the lower bidders—at a price that was $1.5 million less than his estimate. It is likely that the government worked to ensure that a contractor with the proper experience and resources got the work, and they were wise to do this because in Onderdonk they got a good one. Yale to Port Moody came in six years early.

The first contracts covered the route from Emory to Savona, a distance of 127 miles. In the 50 miles up to Cisco there were numerous tunnels to be drilled, and between them the grade often had to be galleried, meaning it was shelved into the rock above the river far below. From simple addition you would expect him to be $1.75 million out of pocket when he finished, but when Onderdonk's syndicate came out of the Fraser Canyon, it was

CPR mainline construction and the Cariboo Road. The twelve-horse outfit on the temporary roadway shows that the railway was not yet complete because as soon as it was finished, the road ceased to be a continuous link between Yale and Ashcroft.

more than $2.5 million short, a very large sum in those days.[4]

Onderdonk was a clever railway engineer and a personable one, and he so impressed the Canadian government's Minister of Railways, Charles Tupper, that when tenders were called on the 85-mile section from Emory westward to Port Moody, and Onderdonk once again failed to be low bidder, he got the contract anyway—he also threatened to pull out otherwise! When his contracts were taken over by the Canadian Pacific Railway east of Savona, the CPR had him building as far as he could get until he met the contractors coming westward. He reached Craigellachie in November 1885. For this 92-mile section he was paid on a cost-plus basis.[5] (See map "The Canadian Pacific Railway from Port Moody to Revelstoke.")

By this time he was in the black, largely because he had a fiery Irishman named Michael Haney at the helm. Big Mike, or the Irish Prince as he was called, hired hundreds more Chinese labourers and drove them mercilessly. (After the canyon work many of them, with the funds they earned so onerously, returned to China to buy land and build homes and to live happily ever after. However, among them were some who were forever changed; they set up their families in China and then returned to British Columbia. Others less fortunate, including those who gambled their wages away, moved on to an opportune gold find at Granite Creek in the Tulameen Valley.[6] Many went to Barkerville; others drifted to coastal centres and laid the roots of Vancouver, Nanaimo, and Victoria Chinatowns. The last-mentioned had a perfectly legal opium factory, one of British Columbia's first ventures in trans-Pacific trade![7])

The advent of Onderdonk and Haney was one of the best things that ever happened for the railway in British Columbia, as it is difficult to see how the job could have been done otherwise. Haney's resourcefulness included a prefabrication scheme for railway trestles and bridge spans, which made it both easier and quicker to place them.[8]

The only group that suffered from all of this, besides the Chinese labourers, was the road authority of British Columbia.

Housing built for Chinese labourers working on the CPR, c. 1883.

Onderdonk destroyed 7.5 miles of the old Cariboo Road, more than half the distance from Yale to the Alexandra Bridge, and he replaced that road with a roadway on flimsy trestles closer to the river that barely outlived the construction period. There was just no way he could do otherwise with the rock-blasting techniques of the time, especially given the time limits imposed on him.

In addition to this he started a process that eventually destroyed 19.5 miles of road east of Lytton in the Thompson River valley between Gladwin and Spences Bridge. This did not happen immediately. It took some time, and involved in it was the delay in finishing the Cisco Bridge. This delay caused a major bottleneck, as work trains could not cross the river at Cisco until the bridge was finished.[9] It was late in 1884 before that happened, and until then the work crews had no locomotives nor rolling stock available beyond it. This meant that the stretch from Cisco to Savona was built with horses and wagons, horse-drawn scrapers, or men with hand shovels and wheelbarrows. Such heavy equipment as they

The CPR bridge at Cisco, near Lytton, was constructed in 1884-5.

did have they had to team up over the wagon roads. Cisco to Spences Bridge was particularly heavy work, with the grade benched into steep slopes of gravel or clay.

The difficulties of construction without heavy equipment could have been avoided for at least six miles if they had stayed on the right bank of the Fraser River between Cisco and Lytton. In terms of engineering challenge there is little to choose between either bank.[10] This would have made things easier for their companion railway 25 years later, and would have saved the Canadian taxpayer the cost of subsidizing two unnecessary railway bridges, as discussed in Chapter 3. It appears the CPR crossed at Cisco because there was convenient terrain to lead into a suitable bridge site from a tunnel at that point, not because there was any particular difficulty about crossing at Lytton.

Jessie Ann Smith, "Widow Smith of Spence's Bridge" according to the title of her memoirs, arrived in Spences Bridge in March 1884 with her new husband, who had come to Britain to marry her. They crossed the Fraser at Cisco in a basket ferry after dismounting from a work train. At that time Andrew Onderdonk and his family were living in Spences Bridge and Jessie became greatly esteemed of "the very lovely Mrs. Onderdonk," as she described her. She wrote, "Our ages were close, and she had younger children, and we became friends almost instantly." She was very sad to see them move on to Savona soon after. Jessie's memoirs also reveal that the grading of the roadbed east of Cisco to Savona at that time was proceeding with concentrated effort, and that many Chinese workers were brought in.[11]

The terrain of the left bank of the Thompson was quite different from that of the right bank of the Fraser from Yale northwards. There were rock outcroppings, but generally the material in the steep hillside was of gravel with sand and silt mixed in. The spectacular rock bluffs in the Thompson Canyon were all on the right bank of the river, a problem later on for the next railway to come on the scene. The cuttings in these hillsides were very difficult to render fully stable due to the lack of compaction in the material. To this day the Trans-Canada Highway and the CPR have constant trouble with boulders rolling down the hillside and, in times of thaw or heavy rain, with slides, and this is with the cuttings widely and fully excavated and in some places protected with chain-link steel mesh.

In 1884 Onderdonk had little chance of doing a complete job in this area, especially without heavy equipment, which could not reach him that year due to the lack of a bridge at Cisco. His cuttings were, therefore, oversteep in their side slopes when he got through with them, and material started falling or sliding onto the railway immediately. All the rail crews could do with this material was "bail it" over the side (as if they were bailing water out of a boat). This meant the rocks and mud landed on the roadway below, but as there was no road traffic, no one complained and it stayed. This destroyed the continuity of the road and made it impossible to maintain. It was at the mercy of the river thereafter, and in the huge flood of 1894 it virtually disappeared. The difficulty of this section was underscored when the road was replaced between Yale and Spences Bridge in 1924 to 1927. Yale to Alexandra Bridge, thought to be the most difficult, went through on time. Gladwin to Spences Bridge was a full year late in completion and cost more than twice the estimate.

The 304 miles of railway that Onderdonk produced from Port Moody to Craigellachie contained a large number of trestles and bridges, over 600 in all. Many of these between Lytton and Spences Bridge were built in a temporary manner—often with unpeeled logs—to save money, and replacement of these by embankments after the railway was in operation in large part destroyed the roadway. Such economies were understandable because both the contractor and the railway flirted with bankruptcy in these years. Those who knew what was going on might have thought that this justified cutting corners, but in the long run it was a poor deal for the province.

Despite all the difficulties, the first train rolled past what was then known as Savona's Ferry late in 1884. (The place name was later shortened to Savona by the railway.) In January 1884 the line had been finished from Port Moody to Emory—construction on this section was helped immensely by the sternwheelers on the lower Fraser. With the section to Savona this made up a total of 212 miles. It was an astounding achievement and Onderdonk and his men deserve nothing but praise for it—except from the road authority for which they left one huge deficiency: no road in the canyon!

How closely Joseph Trutch watched what was going on is not known. He was the ex-Lieutenant-Governor of B.C., the builder of the Alexandra Bridge, and from 1880 to 1889 he was the representative of the dominion government, which let the contract for this stretch of railway. During his time as dominion agent he presided over a sad ending to a wonderful road and bridge. He was a heroic pioneer bridgebuilder, the first to tackle a major river crossing in British Columbia, and it is tragic that he did not manage to assure continuing road access to his bridge.[12] Trutch should have foreseen the problems that would arise from the shortcuts the contractor was taking, but apparently he did not, or else he ignored them.

The Alexandra Suspension Bridge built by Joseph Trutch across the Fraser, showing the west towers and the toll house on the left side of the picture. The bridge was later raised on a sandstone foundation transported from Newcastle Island in Nanaimo Harbour.

THE FAMILY TRUTCH

Joseph William Trutch was a leading figure in commercial and civil engineering circles in early British Columbia. First he built the Alexandra Bridge, which turned out to be a very profitable venture. Then he became the chief commissioner of Lands and Works and surveyor-general of the colony, and when British Columbia joined Canada as a province he became its first Lieutenant-Governor.

During all this time he remained a major shareholder in his bridge and in Spence's bridge, in which he had a lesser interest, despite being the official in both colony and province responsible for administering the charters and permissible rates for toll bridges.

It is reported that when he became the Queen's representative he tried to divest himself of the Alexandra Bridge, along with its toll charter. But his price of $30,000 was too high, even for the government, and he had no takers. He therefore continued to bank his tolls, and he even presided over a revision upward of them during his term.

His wife, whom he met in Oregon before coming to B.C., was the sister-in-law of the surveyor-general of that territory. This connection probably led him to the man in San Francisco responsible for the cables on their trolleys. It was he who supplied the cables for the Alexandra Bridge.

Trutch's sister Caroline came to B.C. and married Peter O'Reilly, the gold commissioner and a member of the Legislative Council. His brother John married the daughter of Governor Musgrave. It was widely believed that these connections helped Trutch gain his appointment as Lieutenant-Governor, although his outstanding contribution to B.C. would have stood him in good stead for that.

After a spell in England he was appointed dominion agent. One of his duties was to oversee the construction of the CPR mainline in B.C. At about that same time his brother John became a senior executive for Andrew Onderdonk, who obtained all the contracts for the building of the CPR from Vancouver to Craigellachie.

Trutch received a knighthood for his service as dominion agent, and after the railway was completed his brother became the dominion government's agent for the administration of the railway lands on Vancouver Island.

There was an excess of engineering talent to assist him, so Trutch had no excuse there. Henry Cambie and Marcus Smith were in the first group of exploring surveyors hired by engineer-in-chief Sanford Fleming when the Canadian government took on the task of finding the route for the railway in the west. Cambie and Smith also worked as construction superintendents for the dominion government. On a civil engineering project the construction superintendent either stakes out the work with his own crew or supervises the contractor doing it (in this case, Onderdonk). The superintendent ensures that the work is done properly and meets the specifications, checks the quantities submitted, and having done this, authorizes the payment. Cambie was the superintendent from Emory to Boston Bar. Then he joined the CPR and worked under its banner from Savona to Shuswap Lake. He was immortalized by a street named after him in Vancouver. Marcus Smith supervised from Port Moody to Emory. He refused to sign the final release for Andrew Onderdonk in October 1884 because he was not satisfied with the standard of work. In the end he was bypassed—he was that kind of man!

The construction superintendent for the work from Shuswap to Craigellachie was none other than Major A.B. Rogers, the American prairie surveyor who considered himself God's gift to the survey phase of the CPR mountain division. His arrogance earned him the dislike of most of his Canadian colleagues. Cambie admired Rogers for his energy, but both he and Smith maintained that it was Walter Moberly's crew chief, Albert Perry, who discovered Rogers Pass, not Rogers. (Moberly first worked with Edgar Dewdney, then became the assistant surveyor-general of the colony before working on the railway.) Smith once referred to Rogers as "a thorough fraud." Rogers' construction crews referred to him as "the Bishop" because of his colourful language. He did have one thing going for him: the strong support of the general manager, William Cornelius Van Horne, the American who was brought in to build the CPR.

AN OVERLAND COACH ROAD TO CANADA

Walter Moberly, an Upper Canada-trained railway engineer, arrived in B.C. in 1858 to survey roads and trails. With Edgar Dewdney he took a contract for "a good mule road to the Similkameen," as the first part of the Dewdney Trail was originally called, although they only got as far as the headwaters of Whipsaw Creek. After going bankrupt while honouring a Cariboo Road contract, he became assistant surveyor-general to Joseph Trutch, Colonel Richard Moody's successor as surveyor-general and Chief Commissioner of Lands and Works for the new colony.

In this job he assigned Dewdney the task of completing the trail that was named after him. All Moberly earned was oblivion when his position was abolished in 1866, and he left the colony. Before that he had spent two wonderful seasons surveying a route through the Selkirks and the Rockies for a coach road out of the colony towards the new nation called Canada to the east. It was important that residents of British Columbia be able to reach this nation without having to go into the United States.

Trutch wrote a masterful Minute to the Colonial Assembly in 1868 titled "An Overland Coach Road to Canada," describing three viable routes (see Appendix II). The chosen one was by the Cariboo Road and its connection from Cache Creek to Savona; by sternwheeler to Eagle Pass Landing (now Sicamous); through Eagle Pass (which Moberly discovered) to Big Eddy, now named Revelstoke; by the Columbia River around its Big Bend; through Howse Pass to the navigable North Saskatchewan River; and by it and the Saskatchewan River, again by sternwheeler, to Lake Winnipeg. It was called a coach road rather than a wagon road because it was not meant for transporting goods, only people. It was much easier to transfer a person from stagecoach to river or lake craft and back than it was to switch goods between different conveyances.

While searching for a pass through the Selkirks in 1866, Moberly's assistant, Albert Perry, came within a day's trek of finding Rogers Pass. He reported anticipating a divide at the head of the Illecillewaet River after he abandoned his survey in difficult going. Moberly, probably to avoid criticism for his retreat, wrote in his journal that there was no pass. By that action he discredited his later claim that he discovered Rogers Pass before Major A.B. Rogers. Rogers certainly was assisted in 1881 by Moberly's journal. That Perry got close was supported by the discovery of an old campsite near the summit at the time Rogers claimed he found the pass. The origin of the old campsite, which was discovered by Rogers' crew, was never explained.

The Honourable George Anthony Walkem was premier from early 1874 to early 1876, and again from mid-1878 to mid-1882. During both spells in office he was obsessed with the idea that the railway should go through the Cariboo, down the Homathko River to Bute Inlet, and across Discovery Passage to Vancouver Island (he was a lawyer from the Cariboo). He was so upset when this did not happen during his last term as premier that he vindictively applied a $10 per ton tax on road hauls through the Fraser Canyon. It seems his rage overcame any thoughtful consideration of the best interests of his constituents. As a result, Andrew Onderdonk brought in the Skuzzy to outwit him. Walkem's brother Charles was a surveyor with the CPR and his nephew became the chief of the Cook's Ferry Indian Band when the former chief was killed in the Great Slide of 1905 at Spences Bridge.

Although the construction through the Fraser Canyon was a nightmare, there was one factor in the CPR's favour. Onderdonk's men had convenient access to their railway grade. First the Cariboo Road, then the Upper Thompson River (where they had the reincarnated *Skuzzy*, the *Skuzzy II)*, then Kamloops Lake and the South Thompson and Shuswap Lake with their rivercraft. Haney surely used the latter to move his prefabricated bridge parts and other materials such as rails. Once they got to Sicamous, however, they were faced with the roadless wilderness through Eagle Pass. But even here they had luck.

Early in 1883 there was a new premier in the province, William Smithe, who came on the scene at the end of January.[13] George Anthony Walkem had been premier before him and was no friend of the dominion government and its railway. He had threatened to pull the province out of confederation if the railway was not built down Bute Inlet and across to Vancouver Island. When the government ignored him he

The Honourable Joseph William Trutch (upper left), who lived to the age of 98, was a Legislative Member of the colony of B.C. and deeply involved in the confederation debate and negotiations. He became the first Lieutenant-Governor of the province, serving until 1876.

Major A.B. Rogers (upper right) was the surveyor who defined the route and the location of the CPR transcontinental line across the Rockies and was contract supervisor for the Shuswap Lake to Craigellachie section.

Walter Moberly (lower left), former assistant surveyor-general for the Colony of British Columbia, was the supervising engineer for the first location survey of the CPR transcontinental line in southern B.C.

The Honourable William Smithe (lower right) was premier of British Columbia from 1883 to 1887.

took his revenge by imposing a totally unfair road toll of $10 per ton of freight carried on the public road in the canyon. This led to Onderdonk building and operating his sternwheeler, the *Skuzzy*, to avoid the toll above Yale.[14]

Smithe turned out to be a very good friend to the CPR and he continued to be an ally despite being outmanoeuvred by Van Horne into giving the CPR over 6000 acres of prime waterfront land free of charge on the totally false premise that otherwise the company would place its western terminus at Port Moody. (The CPR would have had to move from Port Moody in any case in order to attain deep-water docking for ocean-going vessels.) The land grant was on the southern shore of Burrard Inlet, containing much of present-day Vancouver's waterfront.

The friendly premier went even further, agreeing to the CPR's demand that Hastings Mill and other businesses occupying the waterfront hand over another 4000 acres to the railway from their crown leases (in each case a third of their holding). This real estate treasure trove on the shores of one of the nation's finest harbours, tax free for twenty years, gave the CPR an edge on the marine shipping market in British Columbia, both coastal and overseas, for many years to come.[15] At the same time the CPR received another gift, a provincial subsidy to build a line from Port Moody to New Westminster, so its cup of happiness was full.

Smithe showed just how good a well-wisher he was during his first legislative session when he introduced an Act to give Gustavus Blin Wright, the creator of much of the Cariboo Road, a roadbuilding deal from Sicamous to Revelstoke in exchange for 60,000 acres of prime crown land (which he could sell in 160-acre parcels).[16] Possibly the CPR had discussed such a project with the province, the authority for roads. And if you wanted a road in a hurry, who better to talk to than Gus Wright, the great roadbuilder from the Cariboo? If you were short of cash, what better to deal in than land?

Wright went ahead immediately and completed the 45 miles through Eagle Pass, midway between Sicamous and Revelstoke,

Gustavus Blin Wright was a genuine hero to road users in the early days of the province. Besides building hundreds of miles of B.C.'s first roads as well as a ferry across the Columbia, he also built the province's most durable sternwheeler, the second Enterprise, *which became a link in the Cariboo Road.*

early in 1884, following the line of the railway that was to be built there. He also installed a ferry across the Columbia River.

The cash-strapped premier's road through the wilderness was viewed as a gift to the CPR, a convenient access road to help the railway's construction and speed its completion. Fortunately for Smithe, he died in March 1887, just before the legislative session and the questions it would have brought.

The way was now clear for Onderdonk to head east from Savona. He had the hard-headed Irishman Michael Haney to wield the bullwhip for him, and early in 1885 that human dynamo was in Kamloops. Soon after that tracks were laid to Sicamous. From there, instead of heading out into the untouched wilderness, they had a brand new wagon road alongside the work. By autumn Big Mike was in Craigellachie awaiting James Ross's crew coming from the east. Henry Cambie said in his memoirs that with more rail available they would have gone farther.[17]

The railway construction crews approaching them also enjoyed Premier Smithe's generosity; they used the wagon road alongside their section from Revelstoke westwards as they moved towards the meeting point. The corporate clout of the CPR paid off for all its contractors. Five years after the railway went into business, the road became impassable due to a total lack of maintenance. With it went a convenient and low-level land link for wagon trains between two waterways, the Columbia and the Thompson. In this way the railway made sure it did not have to compete with wagon trains for freight from Sicamous to the Columbia River, just as it had dealt with the situation in the Fraser Canyon, and the province lost an important road through the Gold Range, which it did not get back for many years.

The Sicamous-Revelstoke road had a chequered career. Between 1895 and 1897 it was completely rebuilt with a connection from Sicamous to Salmon Arm, but it again fell into disrepair. The sketch map with the provincial road review for 1902 shows it for a mere six miles west of Craigellachie, referring to it as an old tote road. It was again rebuilt in 1916 and after that it survived any lethal plans the railway might have had for it. Eventually it became part of the Trans-Canada Highway.

Other strange goings-on involved water travel. New Westminster merchants constantly complained that they were being bypassed when supplies for Interior railway construction were ordered. In 1884 they came tantalisingly close to having this market opened to them. If the Cisco bridge had been completed in the spring of 1884, track would have been laid to Savona early in that year, to coincide with the completion of the track from Emory to Port Moody. New Westminster goods could have travelled by train to Savona, then been transferred to the *Peerless*, a sturdy 131-foot sternwheeler owned by Captain John Irving, which had been plying the Thompson and South Thompson Rivers and Shuswap Lake from Savona to Eagle Pass Landing (as Sicamous was called then) since its launching at Kamloops in 1880.[18] From Sicamous, the 45-mile Eagle Pass Wagon Road was ready to carry traffic to Revelstoke. Train, boat, and wagon would have moved their wares east and the New Westminster grocery suppliers would have reaped a bonanza. As many as 5000 men were on the rail construction crews at a centre like Revelstoke in those days.

What did happen was something quite different. The Cisco bridge was not completed until late in 1884,[19] and this gave the perennial and well-hated competitors from Washington territory

The Peerless *is unmistakable with its high, bell-mouthed funnel. This photo was taken in Kamloops in 1885, after the CPR rail line was completed.*

the opportunity to make their move, helped out by certain co-conspirators north of the border. In 1883 a CPR contractor, H.M. McCartney, arranged for Portland boatbuilders Paquet and Smith to construct the sternwheeler *Kootenai* at Little Dalles on the Columbia, 40 miles upstream of Marcus. It was launched on April 2, 1884, joining the barge-pushing steam launch *Alpha*, which had been in service since the year before.

When the *Kootenai* hit the water there were 1500 tons of supplies all ready to load right alongside it, placed there by Marcus, Colville, and Spokane merchants in anticipation of its maiden voyage on May 1. All summer they provided shipments for it to haul up the Columbia River and the Arrow Lakes to the busy construction centre soon to be renamed Revelstoke. The *Kootenai* came to grief in low water near Little Dalles on September 4, 1884, and ended its career, but not before it had enjoyed a good season.[20]

If the CPR bridgebuilders had bestirred themselves properly, not only would it have made their gradebuilding colleagues' job easier on the stretch from Cisco to Savona, but the New Westminster suppliers would have benefitted greatly as well. These

This 1889 view of the main street of Revelstoke was taken at a time when there were no roads leading away from the townsite. This was to the eminent satisfaction of the grand seigneur *of the city, the CPR.*

eager wholesalers were quite ready to put horses and wagons on Gus Wright's road, and a British Columbian source of supply would have been created. Most residents of the new province believed that this was why the road was built in the first place, and why Gus Wright received these 60,000 acres of prime crown land. The Lower Mainland merchants could have moved freight to Spuzzum by rail and from there on by wagon and boat to serve the railway construction along the way. This was only possible if the railway contractor maintained the road from Lytton to Spences Bridge in reasonable shape as the contract required, and of course this was not done.

Both the Cariboo and Eagle Pass roads were used to help in the rail construction and then both fell into disuse and disappeared. The CPR obviously wanted to avoid competition for freight moving through the province. It was also a willing accomplice to merchants south of the border, helping them supply the construction operation. By the time the 1500 tons of supplies were used up and the Cisco bridge was built, the whole thing was over. There is little wonder that the comments of the editor of the Kamloops newspaper, the *Inland Sentinel,* on the operations of the *Kootenai* were vitriolic, almost to the point of being unprintable.[21]

☆   ☆   ☆

Some events trouble the minds of historians, who wonder whether they were planned or if they just happened. Many of these puzzles remain unsolved and one of them is the question of what happened to the Cariboo Road in the Fraser Canyon after the first train from the east rolled into Port Moody. The great majority of the celebrants believed, if they thought about it at all, that there was still a road in existence from Yale to Spences Bridge and from there on to Barkerville and elsewhere in the Interior, and no one in government or in the railway contradicted this belief.

It was not much of a road, however, especially the 13 miles from Yale to Alexandra Bridge, because, as already mentioned, 7.5 miles of it had been totally destroyed by the railway builders and only a very temporary replacement was put in its place. The replacement was primarily for use during the railway construction period, and in the 1894 flood the trestles were all washed out by the river.[22]

No one could blame Onderdonk for not fully exerting himself on this in view of the onerous road toll Premier Walkem had unwisely inflicted upon him. The dominion government quietly

This photograph is from the Andrew Onderdonk album, which mentions five tunnels in five miles, but this photo only shows four. It is upstream of, but close to, Chapman's Bar. There is only one tunnel in this area now, possibly the farthest. Chittenden, in his journal, speaks of the numerous spurs of granite rock north of Yale, which pushed Onderdonk's costs as high as $300,000 a mile, and they are evident here. The river at this point is deep, swift, turbulent, and very dangerous.

This CPR excursion train north of Spuzzum in the Fraser Canyon carried day trippers in open cars. Today it seems foolhardy to come to a standstill in a falling rock area like this even in the best of conditions. There is fractured rock at slopes from 45 degrees to close to vertical.

It took brave men to run these trains. In the winter even a medium-sized snowslide could sweep away the grasshopper trestles.

looked the other way, as it was equally upset with the good premier for other reasons. H.J. Cambie recalls that the CPR had built a number of grasshopper trestles to carry the railway along the same steep rock slopes; they were much more sturdy than those built for the road.[23] This was to save time and money, both being in short supply to the railway builders. These structures were eventually replaced by fills and retaining walls.

There was a good road from Hope to Yale, built by an ex-Royal Engineer, which crossed the Fraser River by ferry. This survived the railway construction quite well.[24] Further west, the section of the Old Yale Road from Hope to Chilliwack was a continuing problem as the Fraser washed it out regularly, but it was there. Beyond the railway incursion at the northern end of the Thompson Canyon, the Cariboo Road continued on its way to Barkerville as it had before, starting from the right bank of the Thompson River at Spences Bridge, where there was a toll bridge. Another road ran east from Spences Bridge to Merritt.

After the railway opened there was little traffic on the road from Yale to Spences Bridge and on to Ashcroft, as the new way to travel, with its lack of dust, superior speed, and smoothness of riding, quickly won over the passenger trade. Terminals for the stagecoaches and for the mule and oxen trains were moved from Yale to Ashcroft. The wagoners moved because the railway rate-setters immediately underbid everyone else on freight charges, a final blow to any use of the canyon road. At Ashcroft, another toll bridge across the Thompson enabled the wagon trains to rejoin the Cariboo Road and head north from the railway.

For this reason there was nothing left but local traffic, and very little of that, for the road from Yale to Ashcroft.[25] There was also an apparent lack of interest on the part of any higher authority in the Department of Lands and Works to maintain the historic road that had been their first love, one more indication of the enchantment with railways that seemed to have come to almost every British Columbian at the time.

The road authority still felt the same way 25 years later, as was proven by its response to a request from the Canadian Northern Pacific Railway (later the Canadian National) in 1910 to demolish what was left of the old road on the left bank of the river as work commenced on the second railway through the Fraser Canyon. Permission for the second phase of the destruction of this section of the Cariboo Road came in a letter from Public Works Minister Thomas Taylor to Public Works Engineer F.C. Gamble dated July 6, 1910.[26] It read:

> It is not the intention to rebuild the old wagon road, nor to rebuild the bridge at Spuzzum.

By this decision, any right of compensation to the people of British Columbia for the very severe damage done to Governor James Douglas's masterpiece of roadbuilding by the construction of the CNPR disappeared.

A B.C. Express stagecoach driver stops along the sixteen-foot-wide Cariboo Road. Log cribbing was widely used by the early road builders. As evident, it adjusted itself to any settlement of the road surface.

In fairness, some defence for this lack of political will lies in the fact that the Alexandra Bridge was severely damaged in the 1894 flood. The cable anchors were washed out, resulting in the deck being badly skewed, mostly because nobody cleared out the debris that hung up on the windstay cables underneath, and in the following years the fine old structure was considered a write-off. It was deemed only suitable for travellers on foot or horseback.[27]

A report by Public Works Engineer Gamble to Minister Taylor in 1910 shines some more light on the subject. Gamble was close to retirement in that year and had been present throughout the railway construction. He wrote:

> Since the opening of the C.P.R. the Government has abandoned the Yale-Cariboo Road between Yale and Spuzzum, and between the suspension bridge, which cannot be repaired, and Boston Bar, and consequently it has become impassable and practically non-existent. It is used only by Indians on foot or horseback, who have made trails around the slides or cave-ins, etc.[28]

Assistant Public Works Engineer G.P. Napier put out an excellent report twelve years after this in which he stated that the original contract with Onderdonk required him "to keep all public and private roads in such condition as to be safe and convenient for the public." He said that he had studied the earlier correspondence in the files and found that Joseph Trutch had insisted that Nick Black, former road superintendent at Yale, be appointed to ensure that any diversions were carried out satisfactorily. Napier then reports that this was not done, likely because Black, who had given stalwart service for many years following the opening of the Cariboo Road, had retired by the time the railway was built. In Napier's words, the road was "mostly ledges in the rock connected by grasshopper trestles, all of which were too low for the 1894 flood which washed out all the trestles."

Black was replaced by a Mr. Sutherland, who was quoted in Gamble's 1910 report confirming that he had been present when Onderdonk rebuilt the road on flimsy grasshopper trestles after it was taken out by the railway. His description of the Alexandra Bridge in 1910 was two words: *no good.* He cut the cables the next year.[29]

Even if Trutch had succeeded in reinstating Black to monitor the road diversions and replacement, he could not have done much to restore the road to its former condition. Anyone on the road in the spring of 1876 would have realised that the grasshopper trestles of the replacement road between Yale and Spuzzum could not withstand a flood. Evidence in the Department of Lands and Works files shows that the river level in that year was just as high as it was in 1894, and that flood washed them out.[30] What was needed was very determined action by the provincial government, but at that time the politicians were so anxious to see the railway completed that no one was prepared to move heaven and earth about a road. After the railway opened, the road's restoration demanded long-term planning, and politicians have never excelled at that.

And there remain questions about whether the closure of the road was intended all along. In his biography of Henry Cambie, Noel Robinson quotes him as saying:

> One of our great troubles was the old wagon road which ran for miles alongside the railway and which had to be kept open as it was the only means of access to the upper country and continued so until the railway took its place.[31]

This implies that there had never been any intention of keeping the road open after the railway was built, despite the clause in the railway contract requiring the contractor "to keep all public and private roads in such a condition as to be safe and convenient to the public." The provincial government gives the game away again in a press release put out in 1913 to explain why it was permitting the CNPR to destroy the Cariboo Road on the other bank of the Fraser (see Appendix I). In the release is a comment about the destruction of the road in the 1880s.

> It was determined at the time that the road could not again be thrown open to traffic.

Intentionally or otherwise, when the railroad was finished, destruction of the wagon road continued. After 1886 the CPR started replacing the railway's temporary trestles alongside the Thompson River with fills. They did this economically by side-dumping from railcars, a process where cars are parked on the track and their contents are either tipped or shovelled over the edge. In many places the fill spilled onto what was left of the wagon road below. As well, as mentioned earlier, there was the continuous problem of boulders, gravel, and silt that slid down and plagued the railway. The CPR found the easiest way to solve this problem was to push the slide material over the side, again onto the wagon road, or else use it as fill to replace the temporary trestles.

But the real clincher for the road in the canyon came with the disastrous floods of 1894. The railway was too busy with its own problems, even if it had cared, and neither the inaccessible sections along the banks of the Thompson River nor the flimsy road trestles between Yale and Spuzzum received any attention at all. Sections of the road and the trestles disappeared into the river, and alongside the Thompson the washouts were up to 80 feet in height.

After 1894 the road was simply not there in places, which was probably why they reopened the old Port Douglas to Lillooet alternative. It was quite unsuccessful and soon fell back into disrepair, so all wheeled movement to the Interior was by rail.

Because the provincial government failed to require it to make good the damage to the Cariboo Road, the CPR was totally successful in eliminating any competition from road traffic from the coast to the Interior of the province, unless it passed through the United States. That situation remained in effect until the Fraser Canyon Highway opened in 1927.

The final verdict on the CPR's contempt for the roadway below it was delivered in a report by District Engineer W.G. Gwyer of August 14, 1919, in which he states that the final 19.5 miles into Spences Bridge from Lytton were "practically entirely destroyed by the CPR."[32] The blame for that must go to the two governments involved, provincial and federal, neither of which acted to sustain it.

Gwyer's review of the damage, which was accompanied by a plan prepared by F.J. Dawson in February 1920, compared two alternatives: replacing the canyon road or building a new road from Hope to Princeton. Gwyer estimated the cost of the damage at $375,000 for 38.5 miles of road. He deducted this from his cost estimate for a new road in the canyon as he expected the CPR would reimburse the province in like amount, which did not happen. With this deduction the cost of rebuilding in the canyon would have been less than new construction from Hope to Princeton. Gwyer commented in his report that the Hope-Princeton route would be open in the summer months only. He obviously hoped that the result of all this would be a rebuilding through the canyon, and it was.[33]

An earlier assessment of the damage in dollars was made in 1910, when attempts to settle for compensation between the CPR and the province commenced. These negotiations turned out to be a farce, one that went on sporadically for fifteen years. In the end, the railway agreed to pay $1000 for every public road crossing, the logic of which was undetectable. The CPR paid only for damage from Cisco eastwards because west of that the tracks had been laid under a federal government contract.

Evidently the rail line crossed the road 26 times between Cisco and Spences Bridge, so the railway paid the princely sum of $26,000 for the havoc it wrought along the Thompson River valley. It paid another $15,000 for four miles wiped out as well as for other casting damage, and $4000 for a railway crossing wrongly filled in. This amounted to $45,000 for the damage to the Cariboo Road between Lytton and Spences Bridge: damage that towards the end of these negotiations had been carefully assessed by Gwyer as worth $131,000. In addition the railway had to build a pedestrian subway under the track at Lytton.[34]

The CPR also won a continuing concession: for every railway crossing it allowed in future it would receive $1000! The logic in this is also undetectable. It gave the railway precedence at all crossings and meant that anyone subsequently seeking to cross the track would have to pay all costs and could not in any way infringe on the CPR's right-of-way without the consent of the railway. This applied to the provincial government as well as individual users.[35] Considering that the road authority had been there first, which is the definition of precedence, the CPR's clout in Ottawa worked out well for the railway in this. Its negotiators must have smiled as they left the table.

When the province finally got around to replacing the canyon road in the 1920s, provincial finances were sorely stretched by the construction of more than 2000 feet of retaining wall necessary to support the road alongside the Thompson River near Nicomen Creek. The railway, located above the road, was an equal beneficiary of this river-edge revetment but in spite of this, and despite its neglect making the replacement of the bank necessary in the first place, the CPR did not contribute a nickel. Bill Gwyer thought that they should have paid for every foot of it.

All in all, the fate of the Cariboo Road in the Fraser Canyon and in the Thompson Canyon from Lytton to Spences Bridge is a sad story. The passing of the grand old road was forgotten quickly in the joy of the new and convenient mode of transportation. Foresight that something could be said for keeping a road there extended only as far as a rather vague clause in Onderdonk's contract that "public and private roads be kept in a condition convenient to the public." As can be seen, the supposed guardian of the public, Henry Cambie, the construction engineer supervising the contractor, an excellent man otherwise, seems to have missed the point—unless he felt that "the convenience of the public" could never be better served than by the railway!

In the story to come in Chapter 3, the possibility of resurrecting the road was put in further jeopardy by the building of a second railway in the same canyons. The file on the road's demise grew thicker and thicker before the province finally got the bit in its teeth and put things to right.

Chapter 3

Hope to Kamloops Again

A second railway trades sides with the first in the Fraser and Thompson Canyons, and a replacement roadway loses out in the shuffle

William Mackenzie and Donald Mann are in some ways the mystery men of Canadian railways as their names keep cropping up in odd places. To Canadian railway historians and to all proponents of the iron road they are heroes indeed. Both were native-born Ontarians involved in Canada's first national railway

Sir William Mackenzie (left) and Sir Donald Mann (right). These two railway tycoons were gloriously Canadian in an era when most of their ilk were Americans. Unfortunately they dimmed their radiance by manipulating politicians throughout their careers.

adventure right from the very start. They ended up at Craigellachie as remarkably successful mountain contractors, operating independently. Their success came from cunning, skill, diligence, and tough-mindedness, traits both possessed in no small measure.

After the first transnational line was complete, Canada's railways took off. Over the next ten years there was the extension of the CPR—for example, the B.C. southern line to the Kootenays— and also the creation of other networks to serve the eastern and central provinces, specifically the Grand Trunk and the Canadian Northern.

Through their involvement with the last-mentioned, in which they entered into a lasting partnership, Mackenzie and Mann became masters of the art of inveigling politicians to build railways practically anywhere—at the drop of a hat or the rattle of a gold pan.[1] This skill blossomed in North America during the late nineteenth century. Mackenzie and Mann, pioneers in the field, served their apprenticeship by persuading the settlers of Manitoba to donate labour to build spur tracks from their neighbourhood grain elevators to what was described as "a 100 mile long line of no consequence" proceeding westwards from Winnipeg to Saskatchewan. Despite the insult, which probably originated with the CPR, this line was an asset that every farming group desired. It was the Canadian Northern Railway. With local and provincial governments pressing free labour and land and many other benefits on them in return for rail lines, and thanks to their easy ability with words, Mackenzie and Mann did very well and their bank accounts grew accordingly.

The Klondike gold rush brought them out to the West Coast in 1897. They knew instinctively that mining politicians' dreams of iron roads was a much easier way to acquire gold than digging in the frozen gravel alongside Bonanza Creek. Quickly they persuaded B.C. Premier John Herbert Turner to subsidize their plan to build a railway grade from Stewart northwards to Teslin Lake. At the same time they started work from the lake southwards. The next year the CPR and the government in Ottawa got into

The Honourable John Herbert Turner was premier of British Columbia from 1895 to 1898.

the act; the southern terminus was shifted to Telegraph Creek and a steamboat was built on Teslin Lake, this waterborne addition being financed by the dominion government.[2]

The first of these proposed routes to the gold fields was stopped dead in its tracks after 40 miles were built out of Stewart and up the Bear River valley to the Bear Glacier, which they could not get around, over, or through. Some time later the second route, the rail line from Telegraph Creek (another venture involving Mackenzie and Mann), was also dropped before it even got off the drawing board. All of it became inconsequential when Michael Haney and the White Pass and Yukon Railway stole their thunder.

Governments did not seem to learn much from this reckless expenditure of taxpayers' money. Even while they were still involved with the northern route, Mackenzie and Mann saw the possibility of making money with a route into the Kootenays, where valuable mineral resources had been discovered. Turner granted them a contract to build a railway from the coast to Midway, between Penticton and Robson, but they only had time to grade four miles east of Penticton before Turner lost an election to Charles Semlin and the contract was cancelled. Mackenzie and Mann left the province.[3]

They never gave up, however, and when a new transcontinental rail route to Prince Rupert was announced by Canadian Prime Minister Sir Wilfrid Laurier in 1903, they got over their disappointment that their friend A.G. Blair, Minister of Railways, did not get it for them and kept their eyes on B.C.'s new premier Richard McBride, whom they intuitively regarded as good for at least one more railway across the province. A few years later this was shown to be the case. (A.G. Blair resigned when the northern rail route was awarded to the Grand Trunk Railway and not to the Canadian Northern Railway of his friends Mackenzie and Mann.)

Mackenzie and Mann were clever, and they knew that a politician's greatest desire was to stay in office. Any believable threat to political longevity, when explained to a politician, would gain immediate attention; a solution to the threat, when accepted,

Sir Richard McBride, premier of British Columbia from 1903 to 1915.

would receive sincere support, gratitude, and loyalty. If credit for the solution could be attached to the politician in the public eye, the rewards were even more generous. And once extended, the politician's loyalty would almost never be withdrawn, even if the saviour turned out to be a charlatan, because no politician would ever admit publicly that he was wrong.

Premier McBride's political problem was unease in the minds of Lower Mainland voters about the Grand Trunk Pacific Railway being built to the coast in the north. They feared that Vancouver would lose pre-eminence to Prince Rupert, which was 250 miles closer to the emerging Far East markets, had an excellent harbour, and would soon have a railway that crossed the Rockies via gentle Yellowhead Pass, which was not subject to the heavy snowfall of the south. Kicking Horse and Rogers Passes had demonstrated to the CPR that year-round use could be hazardous. Until the Connaught Tunnel was built in Rogers Pass in 1916, that way through the mountains turned out to be downright dangerous and subject to lengthy closures.

Mackenzie and Mann lost no time in convincing Premier McBride that the solution to this threat was for them to connect their Canadian Northern network in central and eastern Canada to Vancouver, using the Yellowhead Pass and going by way of the Fraser Canyon. This B.C. section would be known as the Canadian Northern Pacific (CNPR). They also encouraged him to take all the credit for this wonderful undertaking. McBride bought it right down to the last spike. His gratitude was undying and his loyalty to them from then on was unending.

When the premier announced the second railway and added that the province was supporting it financially, two of his cabinet ministers resigned. Robert Garnet Tatlow, Minister of Finance, a Vancouver businessman and an excellent administrator, told his premier well in advance that provincial funding to Mackenzie and Mann was neither necessary nor advisable. When his advice was ignored he resigned. He died a few months later.[4]

Frederick John Fulton, McBride's Minister of Lands, also handed in his resignation when he heard that a second railway would be built through the Fraser Canyon. He represented the Kamloops constituency and he had been pushing hard for not just a replacement of the original wagon road through the Fraser and Thompson Canyons but for something better; something suitable for the new vehicle that had come upon the scene. Automobiles had upset the balance: railways were no longer everything. The use of the new horseless carriage had blossomed in Canada, and enthusiasts from eastern Canada headed out sporadically across the nation bound for the Pacific coast, crossing B.C. with the greatest of difficulty. They had to ship their cars by rail for the last leg, and Fulton wanted an end to that.

While someone of lesser character would have settled for the spoils of a major railbuilding operation in their constituency, Fulton resigned on principle. He must have done it with regret because he was a good friend of McBride, and his departure meant the loss of an excellent legislator. As the last Chief Commissioner of Lands and Works (before the department was split into two ministries: Lands and Public Works), Fulton had written the Highway Act, one of the best statutes ever introduced in British

Columbia. His thanks for this from the government was its abandonment of the road that meant everything to him. He ran for the federal parliament and gained election to Ottawa, and his family became a dynasty in Canadian politics.[5]

There was a fourth player in this drama besides McBride, Tatlow, and Fulton. He was Thomas "Good Roads" Taylor, McBride's Minister of Public Works, the nickname coming from his support of the Canadian Good Roads Association before he was handed the job of realizing its goals. What he really thought of his premier's change of plans never came to light. He and his

Fred Fulton (upper) was B.C.'s last Commissioner of Lands and Works and then the first Minister of Lands in the McBride cabinet when the two functions of Lands and Works were separated. He drafted the first Highway Act for the province.

Robert Garnet Tatlow (lower left) was Minister of Finance and Thomas (Good Roads) Taylor (lower right) was Minister of Public Works and Railways in the McBride government.

department's officials had been working diligently towards rebuilding the Royal Engineers' road through the canyon, and of course the announcement of a second rail line stopped them dead in their tracks. No one at that time considered it was possible to have a road as well as two railways in the canyon.

Taylor should have resigned, but he was having so much fun building roads in every direction that he could not do it. He doubled the mileage of roads in B.C. in six years. The province was booming. McBride was a hero with the voters, which was shown in the election of 1909. Taylor obviously decided to stay with him.

This decision brought problems to the Public Works Minister, who was also the Minister of Railways, not the least of which was the effect of his premier's policies on his own political future. Taylor's constituency was Revelstoke, and he had already alienated himself from most of his voters by setting up house and home in Victoria. Revelstoke was above everything else a railway company town, and the premier had just brought into the province the only competition that company had ever known. Fully as disturbing to his constituents was the route Taylor and McBride chose for the replacement to the Cariboo Road in the Fraser Canyon. This new road would run from Hope to Princeton and on to Crowsnest Pass, a destination many miles from Revelstoke, with a connection north from Princeton to Merritt and Kamloops.

Credit is due Taylor for the energy with which he pressed ahead, particularly with improvements beyond Princeton. One explanation might be that Taylor had written off hopes of re-election in Revelstoke, a conclusion that proved to be well founded when McBride's railway bubble collapsed and all the Conservatives bar none were defeated in 1915. Prior to that, in 1912, McBride had won a second election in triumph and, as the cream on the pudding, had received a knighthood.

Taylor dotted the 'i' in the demise of the road in the canyon with his response to a letter he received from the chief engineer of the new railway early in 1910. The railwayman was preparing to build on the left bank of the Fraser Canyon, where a usable pioneer roadway still existed, and he advised in his letter that he had every intention of obliterating it. He also pointed out that there was no longer a usable bridge leading to it.[6]

The Public Works Minister replied that the government had no further interest in either that road or the bridge, and later in the year the cables on the Alexandra Bridge were cut. The classic structure, a monument to pioneer engineering, had been rendered unsafe by a combination of neglect and the workings of the Fraser River, as related in Chapter 2. By this action the government ended any chance that taxpayers might receive compensation from the CNPR for the road's destruction.

Needless to say, when sanity returned in about fifteen years and railways dimmed into a proper perspective, the province returned to the same ground and replaced the road and the bridge for an amount considerably higher than it would have cost in 1909. By that time both McBride and Taylor were gone from the scene. And in 1913-14, as a result of the railway construction, the Fraser River was partially blocked by a rockslide near Hell's Gate and the B.C. salmon run was disastrously affected for many years.

However, the smooth talking of Mackenzie and Mann had wondrous results—for them at least. Mackenzie and Mann received $10 million from the public purse for their railway's terminal in Vancouver. Except for this, there were no cash payments. The method of support involved the railway company issuing bonds that the government, in this case the provincial one, guaranteed. Often the interest on these bonds was also guaranteed.

As well as the millions of taxpayers' dollars the CNPR received from British Columbia, it is said that the total acreage of land donated by the various governments in Canada to Mackenzie and Mann's railway network equalled the size of Belgium and Holland put together.[7] The CNPR's land agent, a man by the name of Alexander McRae, amassed what was described as a sizeable fortune from dealings in land and became one of the founders of the Comox Logging and Railway Company.

This is one example of Canadian governments in the early 1900s handing over tens of millions of acres of public lands to railways that steadily accumulated larger and larger deficits while some of their officials became millionaires. The only bright spots were that the public got some of it back when they took over the railways, and the individuals concerned were seen to invest at least some of their spoils in Canada.

R.G. Tatlow, who resigned as Finance Minister when the CNPR deal was announced, always said that Mackenzie and Mann could easily have financed the Canadian Northern Pacific Railway without any public financial participation at all. The deal the two arranged with the province shows that Premier McBride was a babe in the woods when dealing with Mackenzie and Mann and should have heeded his Finance Minister. The figure of $35,000 per mile that was used in the negotiations was probably substantially more than required, as costs in the lower Fraser Valley and up the North Thompson Valley and through Yellowhead Pass were not excessive. In the final assessment, these two men involved the Canadian public in over $70 million of financial encumbrance through their activities in railways. The financial practices evident in this deal were those that led to the Great Depression in the United States and Canada, and this public indebtedness added greatly to the agony Canada suffered in the 1930s.

One place where the CNPR did not get off cheaply was the Fraser Canyon, as shown by the map "Two Railways in a Canyon," and therein lies a strange tale of CPR intransigence. The CPR refused its fellow railroaders the benefit of continuing on the same side of the river at Cisco, just before both lines turned off up the Thompson. Why the Canadian Board of Railway Commissioners did not simply instruct the two railways to reach a reasonable and sensible solution has never been explained, but it did not. One compromise would have been for the CNPR to build a line from Cisco north on the west bank, with a bridge across the Fraser at Lytton. Then the two railways could have exchanged sides, the CPR giving the CNPR the track it had been

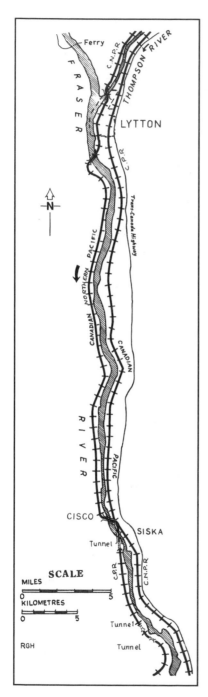

Two Railways in a Canyon

running on and the CNPR turning the new track over to the CPR. The bridge rendered surplus at Cisco would have been available to the CNPR for a crossing of the Thompson River at Lytton. An overhead crossing of one track over the other would have been necessary at that point. Alternatively, both railways could have shared the same side from Cisco to Lytton. The CPR refused this on the basis of one engineer's opinion that the left bank of the river was not sufficiently stable for two tracks. This was proven quite untrue when the Trans-Canada Highway was built. Anything was better than the actual result, which required the CNPR to build two bridges across the Fraser River. This is another example of the massive corporate clout the CPR wielded in Ottawa.

The Board of Railway Commissioners, the arm of the national government that regulated interprovincial railways in Canada, should have asked many questions during these years, but common sense was quickly lost amid the thunder and glory of forging iron links to bind Canada together, and CPR, as the forerunner, was akin to God to many—though not quite everyone!

In 1910, the year after this railway financing fiasco known as the Canadian Northern Pacific Railway was commenced, the perpetrators, Mackenzie and Mann, led a consortium that purchased the Dunsmuir coal interests on Vancouver Island for $11 million (twice their worth). They then turned around and issued a share offering for $25 million. In order to obtain sought-after Canadian Northern Railway bonds, British investors were forced to buy this watered-down stock.

The consortium continued the labour policies of its predecessors, exploiting immigrant workers until forced to do otherwise, and in the course of this they conducted what was probably the most successful strikebreaking operation in Canadian history, one that lasted for almost 25 years.[8]

The Canadian Northern Pacific Railway through the Fraser Canyon and Yellowhead Pass to Edmonton was completed in 1915. Outside B.C., and eventually within the province, it became known as the Canadian Northern Railway. The Canadian Northern was well managed by Mackenzie and Mann, who knew their railways, and except for the interest on its massive indebtedness it would have shown a profit. When that debt reached $400 million in 1917, Prime Minister Robert Borden finally foreclosed and took everything. (The dominion government took control because the province could not handle it and because the railway extended outside the provincial border.) It was reported that the tough railway contractor Sir William Mackenzie broke down and wept.[9]

In 1919 the CNPR became part of the Canadian National system, which also acquired the Grand Trunk Pacific Railway to Prince Rupert.

Chapter 4

Kamloops to Alberta

Trains in the mountain passes are stopped by the deadly snow—and a road takes the long way around because of it

In 1882, as already mentioned in Chapter 1, our friend Newton H. Chittenden made a trip through B.C. At one point he travelled from Savona's Ferry (now Savona) to the Okanagan Mission (now Kelowna) by road, returning to Kamloops by sternwheeler via Fortune's Landing (now Enderby). His route from Kamloops to Kelowna was to Duck & Pringle's (now Monte Creek), from there to Grand Prairie (now Westwold) and Priest's Valley (now Vernon) and Kelowna (and from now on modern names will be used). The waterways he travelled on were the Shuswap River, Shuswap Lake, and the South Thompson River. He describes his trip up the Shuswap (then called the Spallumcheen River) in the *Spallumcheen*, the smallest of three boats on the river then. After an overnight stop on Shuswap Lake he writes, "Salmon and trout were so numerous that I could count them by the dozens from the boat as we advanced in the morning."[1]

Chittenden describes the road from Savona to Kamloops in 1882 as a good to excellent wagon road, though the one from Kamloops to Kelowna was only fair. There was no road from Monte Creek further up the South Thompson at that time, but there was a road from Enderby to Vernon. Chittenden found it took two days' travel on the *Spallumcheen* back to Kamloops (125 miles), with the boat tying up at night. The 75-mile stagecoach

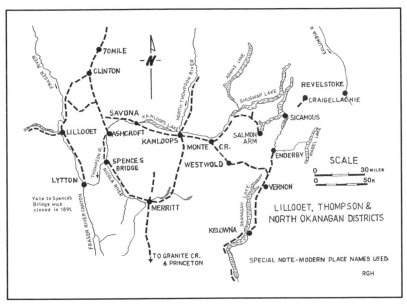

Wagon Roads up to 1902

trip from Kamloops to Vernon also took two days. He then went by road or trail from Kamloops via Nicola (now Merritt) to Cook's Ferry (now Spences Bridge). The route from Kamloops to Spences Bridge he described as a wagon road trail, which was presumably a widened trail, probably fording most creeks.[2]

The total mileage of sternwheeler and lake and river routes shown on the map "Routes of the Sternwheelers" amounts to about 940 miles. Over the next twenty years, as the railways came to and through British Columbia, the status of roads and sternwheelers changed, as was shown by the CPR's treatment of the Cariboo Road in the Fraser Canyon. In 1907 a widely quoted opinion was "The best wagon roads came to be those not in competition with sternwheeler or rail line," but the advent of the automobile changed this outlook very quickly, and the building and improvement of roads accelerated tremendously between 1902 and 1910. In this eight-year period the total mileage of wagon roads in the province went up from 6345 miles to 14,633.[3]

In 1902 the provincial government made a study of all the roads in the Interior in response to a great deal of agitation for

The Peerless, *shown here at the Kamloops steamboat landing in 1885 (it has the highest funnel), was Captain John Irving's first venture into the Thompson River transportation business, in company with local entrepreneurs. The 131-foot-long vessel was launched in 1880. He took command on an exploratory trip down the Thompson River to Spences Bridge and barely made it back. The journey was not repeated. More comfortably,* Peerless *went 100 miles up the North Thompson. It was a powerful vessel capable of 18 knots.*

better roads from a new entrant on the scene, the Good Roads Association. (This organization did great work to justify its name, especially in the first quarter of this century.) The study notes relating to the southern Interior were found in an old Department of Public Works (DPW) file, accompanied by a number of sketch plans for each group of roads, and these have been incorporated into the map "Wagon Roads up to 1902."[4]

The interesting thing about the 1902 review findings is the insight they give to the relationship between the road authority and the railways at that time, as well as the influence of the sternwheelers on the road program. Bearing on the railway's destruction of the Cariboo Road between Lytton and Spences Bridge is the note on the Main Trunk Road, Lytton to Kamloops, in the review. This tells us that after the 1894 flood a trail was scratched back in to serve the local settlers, but it was very difficult to maintain because the railway continued to dump its waste onto the trail. As puzzling as this dumping being allowed is the seemingly passive acceptance of it.[5]

Also relevant is the note on the Craigellachie Road, six miles in length, which is apparently all that was left of the Gustavus Blin Wright road of 1884 from Sicamous to Revelstoke (rebuilt in 1896). This small section was reported as spared from total extinction as a convenience to the settlers on it (some of those who had purchased land from Gus Wright) who were totally dependent on rail to move their produce to market, but who needed the road to accumulate their produce at one point. Later DPW files for this road show that between 1912 and 1915 there was a debate about whether to replace it with a new route by Mabel Lake or to go by the old. The old route won out because Sicamous needed access other than by rail or boat. The road was rebuilt again, for the final time, in 1916.[6]

The Nicola-Princeton Road ran by Granite Creek, the site of an 1885 gold rush, which became a convenient destination for thousands of Onderdonk's Chinese labourers who were turned loose at that time. The town at the mouth of Granite Creek on the Tulameen River burned to the ground in 1907, and the one remaining store and hotel, of a total of thirteen, moved to nearby Coalmont in 1912.[7] About one mile upstream from Granite Creek, Coalmont replaced that town as the local centre after the fire, and the mining turned from gold to coal. As is related in the DPW press release entitled "The Pacific Highway" (see Appendix I), the road was relocated to make way for J.J. Hill's Great Northern Railway in 1910.

The road from Savona eastwards was described in 1925 as a good gravel road with a few miles of pavement into Kamloops. East of that town, except for the first few miles out of town, it was described as "fair, dirt, poor when wet" to within nine miles of Salmon Arm. Then it was good gravel road to Kelowna and a good type gravel road to Penticton. The preferred route from the Okanagan Valley to Kamloops ran along the east side of Okanagan

The gold-rush town of Granite Creek (or Granite City) was one mile upstream from present-day Coalmont. Gold had appeared earlier, but not in quantity until 1885 when the rush was on. The easy gold was gone in one year, although a Chinese community stayed on for many years, eking out a living. Most buildings went up in smoke on April 4, 1907.

Lake. This road carried heavy traffic in farm produce, particularly between Vernon and Kelowna. The 1902 DPW review confirms that the road along the west side of Okanagan Lake, which they seemed to have difficulty naming, was a disaster due to its poor width and alignment.[8] The railways built in that period, including two between Kamloops and Okanagan Lake, rather mysteriously discouraged road improvement. In fact the road east of Kamloops in 1925 appeared to be much lower in standard than it was in 1902.[9]

A combination of the sternwheeler service available on the Thompson and South Thompson rivers and Shuswap Lake, and the completion of the CPR main line delayed the building of the difficult stretch of lakeside road from Salmon Arm to Sicamous until 1931. The sternwheelers aided railway construction in this section, and the boats went on to survive competition from the railway for many years as they served the roadless communities on the north side of the river and around Shuswap Lake. The completion of the CNPR in 1915 spelled the death knell of most of them, including one with the uninspiring name *Distributor*, built specifically to assist the railwaymen. Both the new railway and the increase in road mileage (including the building of a road up the North Thompson valley) took away business, and finally they were all beached.

One of them rose from the grave, however, and was destined to convey a very considerable embarrassment to the Department of Public Works, more particularly to A.L. Carruthers, the bridge engineer. The *C.R. Lamb* was indeed out of action at one point, but it was very much alive within the brain of a certain Captain

The Distributor *is here being relaunched onto the Thompson River. This vessel was built in Victoria to assist in the construction of the Grand Trunk Pacific Railway at Prince Rupert. When that use was over it was brought to the lower coast, dismantled, and shipped to the Thompson River to help in the construction of the Canadian Northern Railway. Its sister ships, the* Conveyor *and the* Operator, *were similarly transferred to Tete Jaune Cache to help the GTP there. They were large and powerful vessels with high-pressure steam engines, well able to carry heavy railway equipment. Their major defect was the unimaginativeness of their names.*

William Louie of Kamloops.[10] He concluded that by purchasing this boat at a low price he could provide cheap transportation for vegetables from the riverside and lakeshore gardens run by Chinese people east of town and around Shuswap Lake.

The C.R. Lamb *came to be owned by Captain Louie in 1933. He bought it cheaply as the sellers thought he would scrap it, as was the fate of all its sister ships on the Thompson. Instead he hauled vegetables with it for 15 years. Like the* Skeena, *the ship died with its master.*

All through the cold and dreary winter of 1932 the sternwheelers lay ghostly quiet and deserted on the beach, including the *C.R. Lamb.* No wonder the DPW got the idea that the paddlewheeler days were over, and the Bridge Branch of the Department laboured mightily throughout the freezing weather to build a low-level bridge across the South Thompson River at Pritchard, working off the ice. Pritchard is eight miles upstream of Monte Creek on the right bank of the river. With the spring and Captain Louie's purchase came his rather casual public announcement that as soon as the DPW moved their bridge out of his way, he would be in business.[11] The Department, which had evidently neglected to acquire senior government approval to block navigable waters, had to move quickly and modify the bridge to include a small lift span.

As evident in the above, the new road that was eventually built in the Fraser Canyon also had tunnels, and they were two lanes wide. Roadbuilders used the excavated rock for masonry retaining walls to replace the timber cribbings, which in this case held the road up above Hells Gate.

The *C.R. Lamb* plied its trade until 1948. The real cost of Louie's vegetables to the public included modification to the bridge and staff to attend and raise the lift span when necessary.

Getting back to road building, in 1922 construction began on the road from Yale to Spences Bridge, replacing the Fraser Canyon section of the Cariboo Road from the 1860s. This decision by the politicians and the Department of Public Works eleven years after they thought it impossible was probably due to the advance of the internal combustion engine, hastened on by World War I and by the general desire for more automobiles, which led to public pressure on the politicians. In the case of the DPW, the pressure seemed to come in the form of their excellent civil engineer, W.G. Gwyer, who had arrived from the CNPR willing to prove that a road could be built through the canyons.

At the same time further east, demand arose for a road connection between Revelstoke and Golden, intensifying as the Fraser Canyon work drew closer to completion. Much of *this* pressure came from two organizations: the Vancouver Board of Trade and the British Columbia Automobile Association.[12]

There was local interest in communities near the proposed road, but in this there were offsetting factors. Revelstoke was a railway town through and through, and the well-being of the iron road prevailed there over anything else. Residents were suspicious of roads. Besides, there was already a road from the west to their town, which was all they really wanted.

Golden was not quite so single-minded. In July 1927 it acquired a road connection to Lake Louise and it also had an improved road south to Cranbrook. For that residents could thank J.H. King, MLA for Cranbrook and Minister of Public Works in British Columbia from 1916 to 1922, who successfully obtained money for roads, especially for the East Kootenay and Upper Columbia areas.[13]

Kamloops, the centre of dissatisfaction with roads in the Interior in these days, had just received its long-sought road link to the Lower Mainland, so the residents of that centre might be considered reasonably content for the time being. By 1927, when the long-awaited Yale to Spences Bridge road and the Lake Louise to Golden road (a joint project of the DPW and the Canada Parks Branch[14]) were opened, the network of roads stretched almost across the province. The map "From Wagons to Motor Trucks" shows the road network in the province in the fall of 1925.

Everyone thought that the same roadbuilders who had done such a good job from Lake Louise westwards would simply continue moving west and complete the link from Golden to Revelstoke alongside the railway through Rogers Pass, only 48 miles as the crow flies from Kicking Horse Pass. But nothing happened.

When faced with a negative decision that will affect voters, politicians seldom act quickly, and it was well into October 1929,

This early rail bridge at Revelstoke included precautionary propping under the main spans—evidently to permit the passage of a full-sized train—that brought problems for waterborne traffic.

28 months later, before Ottawa finally bit the bullet and told British Columbians that there would be no direct highway link across the Selkirks by Rogers Pass. The reason given was, of all things, the difficulty of ploughing snow. The federal government instead proposed a 50/50 split with the province to build around the big bend of the Columbia River, a route that put an extra 108 miles into the trip. There were to be two legs to the project, separated by a crossing of the Columbia at Boat Encampment. The road would follow the right bank of the river from Golden to the bridge site, then cross over and follow the left bank to Revelstoke. Ottawa would build the bridge. The sections were almost identical in length, but there was an existing road for eighteen miles from Golden to Donald, which Ottawa originally declined to upgrade but finally shared in cost.[15]

Ottawa notified Victoria of this proposal in a telegram dated October 4, 1929, from the Minister of the Interior, Charles Stewart, in Ottawa, to Nelson Seymour Lougheed, Minister of Public Works, in Victoria, which said:

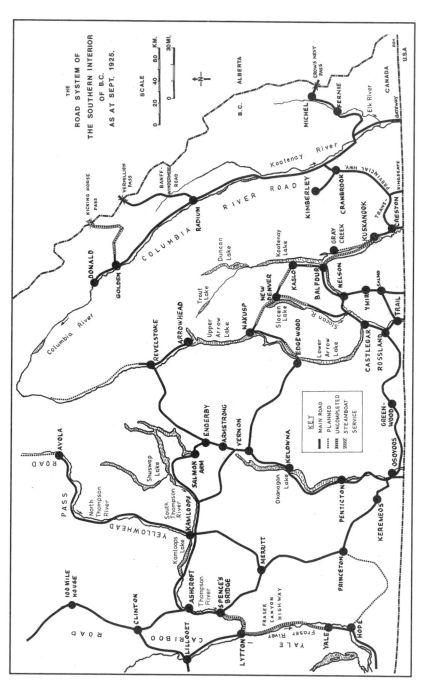

From Wagons to Motor Trucks

The cost of construction of the east leg, from Donald, is estimated at $850,000. If B.C. will complete the west leg by the end of 1932, the Dominion will complete the east leg by the same date. Immediately after hearing of your acceptance we will commence this fall.

Stepping back a few paragraphs, the reader may ask why the expression "of all things the difficulty of ploughing snow" was used. The answer is that in 1927, when these two highway sections were opened—Yale to Spences Bridge and Golden to Lake Louise—neither the provincial nor the dominion government had any intention of keeping either one of them open in winter. With the technology of the time they did not have the capability to plough roads in heavy snowfall areas, nor did they have such things as anti-freeze, and it would be well into the 1930s before they did. Steam power on rails could make a try at it and had done so, sometimes disastrously, but there was nothing on the roads then to do the job. This had not deterred the government from building roads in heavy snowfall areas up until then, so for the national government to use it as a reason to reject the use of Rogers Pass for a road raises questions in the least suspicious of minds. Especially when the result was an extra 108 miles of difficult road travel through undeveloped and rather useless country.

Was there an unrevealed participant in this decision? Probably no one will ever know, but certainly it was not in the best interests of the Canadian Pacific Railway to encourage any more competition in the hauling of freight through the mountains of British Columbia, especially considering that it had just received the company of a road in the Fraser Canyon. The CPR had never hesitated to approach politicians in the past for help, so why not here, when it was faced with even more competition, even if it was only in the snow-free months?

In contrast, the road through Kicking Horse Pass was vital for Canada's Parks Branch's plans to develop the wonderful new parklands in the Rocky Mountains. The railway would have had little success with any opposition there, so the best opportunity to slow the trucking industry lay in the denial of Rogers Pass for road use; an unkind supposition but nonetheless quite possibly a true one considering the CPR's past record.

The view of Rogers Pass from the top of Mount Abbot shows it to be wide and spacious, a prominent feature of the landscape. It is hard to believe that surveyors frequenting the Selkirk Range in the 1870s did not discover it, or at least learn of it from the Native peoples, but apparently they did not. It is also hard to believe that the dominion government would deny the provincial government use of such an obvious way through the mountains fifty years later— but they did.

The bus is bound for Lake Louise from Golden on the Parks Branch road between these points—the photograph was taken some years before it became the Trans-Canada Highway. The stream is the Kicking Horse River. Mount Stephen, in the background, shows that the CPR hierarchy had some very impressive mountains named after them.

Mt. Sifton	Multi-peaked Mt. Rogers	Mt. Hermit	Mt Tupper
9,643 ft.	10,536 ft.	10,194 ft.	9,220 ft.

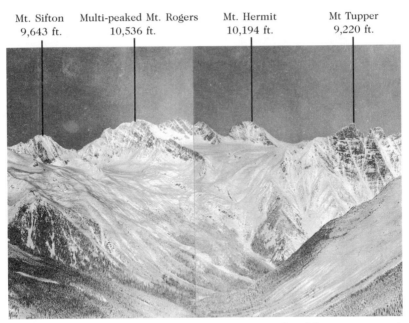

This view of Rogers Pass from Mount Abbot is reproduced from a panoramic photograph by B. Engler.

The three-year construction period suggested by the dominion government for the big bend route was a pipe dream. The railway-men probably realized that, and they knew that any competition they could expect from that quarter would face a lengthy delay. As it turned out, the construction of the road around the big bend took ten years.

It is ironical that the avenue through the mountains that Ottawa deemed suitable for a road, Kicking Horse Pass, was 1294 feet *higher* in elevation than the one it refused to consider and said would be too difficult to snowplough. In addition, the western approach to Kicking Horse Pass was much steeper in slope of land than Rogers Pass, and it quickly became notorious for landslides, debris torrents, and instability.

Just how difficult the terrain leading up to Kicking Horse Pass was has been confirmed over the years, most recently in September 1996 when the Geologic Survey of Canada, in co-ordination with the University of British Columbia, scheduled

THE WRONG PASS

When J.J. Hill stormed out of a Canadian Pacific Railway boardroom in May 1883 over the decision to keep the railway entirely within Canada, the only remaining member of the hierarchy supportive of Hill's protege, Major A.B. Rogers, was his fellow American, William Cornelius Van Horne. It might have been better for Canada if Rogers had left with Hill.

Rogers chose Kicking Horse Pass as the railway's route through the Rockies, and he clung to this choice, even when he must have had doubts about it. Kicking Horse was the wrong pass—they should have used Howse Pass, as Walter Moberly had advocated. By May 1883, CPR track had only reached Medicine Hat from the east. There was still an opportunity to use another crossing of the Rockies.

Rogers' line up the Kicking Horse Valley crossed the face of Mount Stephen 300 feet above the river at the point where Field is today. It required a 1600-foot-long tunnel through the nose of the mountain, and it also crossed two difficult avalanche paths. James Ross, the engineer in charge of construction, rejected the line when he first saw it late in 1883, and he never returned to it. He authorized a survey up the Bow Valley at the last minute, with an eye to going through Howse Pass. This survey showed that they would have to cross Bow Pass, within the Rockies, at an elevation of 6878 feet, and that was impossible. To use Howse Pass properly they would have had to enter from the North Saskatchewan River valley, and by that date CPR trackage was in place for many miles up the Bow Valley past Calgary.

To solve their problem in the Kicking Horse Valley going eastwards, CPR engineers had to reverse their gradient at a point below Mount Stephen, thereafter known as Muskeg Summit, and descend to Field, then climb at a gradient of 4.5 percent (twice that permissible) to Kicking Horse Pass, on a section which was dubbed the Big Hill. The first train to go down it ran away and killed a crew member. The route was a financial drain on the CPR for years, as extra locomotives were needed to haul trains up the Big Hill, and numerous runaway tracks were built in an attempt to make it safe. In 1902 they rerouted around Muskeg Summit for six miles, following the edge of the river, and they finally replaced the four-mile climb up the Big Hill with the spiral tunnels in 1909. These tunnels involved a large amount of hand work with a huge crew, at one time said to be 10,000 men working around the clock for two years.

This was not cheap, but it was a solution to the problem, one which few location engineers would have survived. Rogers blustered through, with the help of Van Horne, and he emerged as a hero.

This shows the short tunnel through the nose of Mount Stephen at the foot of the big hill in the Kicking Horse Valley. A.B. Rogers' survey of the line upon which the railway was to be built came through here about 200 feet higher up. There was to be a 1600-foot tunnel through that seamed and unstable rock. It is little wonder that construction engineer James Ross immediately rejected Rogers' location, an action which resulted in the CPR's having to lay track up the big hill at a gradient twice as steep as that specified.

its annual Slope Hazards Trip for Kicking Horse Pass. In describing this choice the tour organizers wrote:

> Few locations in the Canadian Cordillera present such a variety of slope hazards affecting both a major highway and a railroad...and geological engineering solutions to cope with these problems go back over a hundred years.[16]

Here is a good point at which to consider this problem of snowploughing in high mountain passes with heavy snowfall. The key to success and safety is really quite simple, and it relates to the location of the road or railway in the pass. The grade should never be on the floor of the pass, especially one shaped like a saddle as Rogers is. Instead, the road or rail should be located on the mountainside at an elevation above the floor of the valley of about twice the maximum depth of snow cover expected. As an example, a snowfall of 50 feet over a winter may result in a snow cover on level ground of 20 to 30 feet in depth in the spring, depending upon the rate of snowfall and the temperature fluctuation throughout the winter. In such a case, track or roadway should be located on the hillside at an elevation of 60 feet above the base of the hill so the snow may be ploughed over the outer edge to fall down the slope with ample room to accumulate below the grade.

The rotary snowplough in Rogers Pass on the CPR has its hands or its mouth full! The railways had the only power to throw snow in the early 1900s. Gasoline engines needed anti-freeze; the steam engine did not, and steam had no challenge for many years. If they had located the tracks anywhere else than on the floor of the high snow-trap passes they would have saved lives as these snow walls drift in quickly and a stalled train was at the mercy of avalanches.

If the railway is located on the floor of the pass, as the line in Rogers Pass was originally, and if it is progressively snowploughed throughout a bad winter, in the spring it may find itself running between snowbanks that are 20 to 30 feet high on either side. If a train running between these walls in the pass during a sudden spring blizzard becomes stalled by drifted snow, and if the temperature suddenly rises, the train is in extreme danger from snowslides or avalanches coming down the adjacent mountain slopes. This is exactly what happened in the early days of March 1910, when a train became snowbound and the CPR moved in a large crew to dig it out by hand. An avalanche came down on them and killed 62 men.

The map of Rogers Pass shows the location of the Trans-Canada Highway as completed in 1962.[17] If the dominion Minister of the Interior had permitted a road to be built through Rogers Pass in 1929, it would have followed the same line as the Trans-Canada and would have entered the pass higher up the slope, as the highway does now. (Permissible grades on roads usually exceed those on railways by at least a factor of three, so this construction would have been acceptable.)

In an attempt to make the trackage less hazardous, thousands of feet of wooden snowsheds were built, starting in the 1880s, as the snow hazard became clear. Many of these were made redundant when the Connaught Tunnel was built in 1916, and some near Bear Creek might have been available for road use. Snowsheds are still required in the pass but are of modern design.

The disaster in the spring of 1910 was the one and only reason the dominion government put forward in 1929 to disqualify Rogers Pass for a road. Now we know that road and rail can exist side by side quite happily in that pass, and quite safely provided there is adequate avalanche control, but in 1929 this reluctance cost British Columbia a much-needed road through the pass.

Before looking at the result of that mistake, it should be mentioned that in 1927 a Vancouver consulting engineer by the name of D.O. Lewis examined Rogers Pass, and he announced

In March 1910 the CPR had not yet learned the lesson that a sudden mild spell after a heavy snowfall is a good time to stay away from the floor of a mountain valley. Here searchers dig for victims of the avalanche that killed 62 men of the crew that moved in to clear the track. The bad reputation thus gained by the pass is one reason that a road through Rogers was so late in coming.

This series shows the interiors of CPR's timber snowsheds. Most of these were abandoned when the Connaught Tunnel opened in 1916, and eleven years later the president of the Association of Professional Engineers in B.C. said they should have been used to accommodate a road through Rogers Pass. Van Horne started building 30 snowsheds in 1886 as soon as he realized the avalanche problem in Rogers Pass. The total length of the snowsheds exceeded five miles, they required 17 million board feet of sawn timber and 1.1 million lineal feet of wooden poles and piling, and they cost $1.1 million. The overhead clearance was 22 feet and the width inside was 16 feet. For a two mile stretch in the heart of the pass, Van Horne insisted that a parallel track be built so that the tourists could travel outside and see the glaciers in the summer.

that it was an eminently feasible route for road construction. His report received wide coverage in the Vancouver newspapers, which included his comment that the grade abandoned by the CPR after the Connaught Tunnel went in was quite usable throughout the pass and along the Bear Creek valley.

Lewis reported that because steeper grades were permissible for a road, builders would be able to avoid the avalanche slopes near the pass on the western side, and the road would be perfectly safe. He also noted that there was an abandoned forest company railway grade that could be used to save costs, and he mentioned the surplus snowsheds. It was all good reading for the automobile buffs in the Lower Mainland and on Vancouver Island, and as D.O. Lewis was the first president of the Association of Professional Engineers of B.C., having served in that position in 1921, his opinion was no fly-by-night one, but it was all to no avail.[18] He was ignored.

The best thing that could be said for the big bend route was that it followed a steady river gradient, albeit a rather steep one, and therefore it had no substantial climbing or descending grades. That was about the only saving grace. The valley of the Columbia between Revelstoke and Donald had little value for settlement or for anything other than its timber resources and its excellent water storage capacity. Any mineral wealth had been taken out long before. A road built in that area would run through endless miles of steep slopes of rock and gravel surmounted by trees and little else. The contour slopes steeply to the river, and for its western half the valley is best described as a typical Selkirks V-trench, difficult for roadbuilding (though not impossible). The decision to go ahead round the big bend in 1929 was made despite all of this, and work was under way at each end early in 1930, true to the telegraphed offer made by the national government. The province spent $450,000 that year and the dominion even more.

The following year the depression began to cast its shadow. With unemployment relief workers taking over the work, the provincial Department of Public Works' enthusiasm, output, and expenditure immediately decreased drastically. The Parks Branch made up for this by increasing its contribution, and the overall progress stayed on schedule. In spite of these efforts, the terrible thirties took their toll and 1933 saw very little progress at all on the provincial section, simply because the province was bankrupt.

In 1934 the Canadian Army took over the relief camps and with them all the new road construction of the DPW, such as there was. In a generous gesture the dominion Parks Branch took over work on both legs of the joint project, and by the end of 1937 the roadwork was generally complete except for final surfacing—and except for the bridges on the provincial leg, of which there were many. Finishing these, and carrying out the makeshift sand-on-oil paving that provincial Public Works Minister Charles Sidney Leary insisted upon (which was largely gone in one year), took the final completion date of the highway into the war years.[19]

The Big Bend Highway, when it was finally in full use after the war, had a roadway barely two lanes wide, and when the oil disappeared it was dusty to a degree seldom experienced anywhere. Because of this and its excessive length through undeveloped country, it was never used to its full capacity. There is nothing the average motorist abhors more than a detour, and the Big Bend Highway was a long and dusty detour on the way to Alberta. It required a stout-hearted trucker to take it on, and the tourists mostly went elsewhere. The CPR certainly had nothing to fear from a trucking industry that had to use this road. The fact that it was finished at all was largely due to the Canada Parks Branch, which built its section in excellent fashion and on time, an achievement the B.C. Department of Public Works did not match.

In 1952, twelve years after the Big Bend Highway was opened, a group of highway location engineers of the DPW made an investigation to decide whether the existing route between Revelstoke and Golden should be improved to Trans-Canada Highway standards or whether a new route through the Selkirks should be chosen.[20] These men probably knew as much about locating and constructing highways in difficult mountain terrain as any who could be found in Canada. With the surge of catching-up that had followed the world conflict, the provincial road authority in British Columbia had developed an expertise in road design in mountainous terrain that could only be described as unique, certainly in North America.[21] It is significant that when road design and construction commenced in the national parks, Ottawa employed one of these engineers to be in charge.

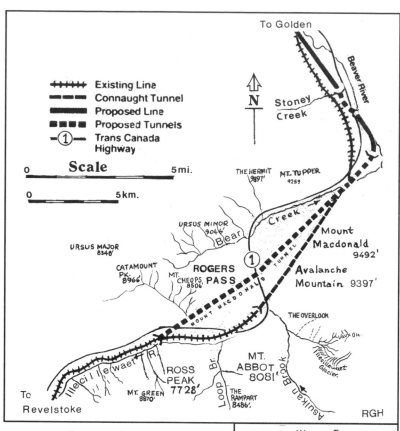

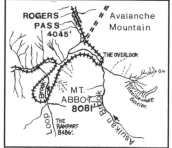

Rogers Pass

This map shows the CPR mainline and the additional line and tunnel constructed in 1984. It also shows the Trans-Canada Highway. The Mount Macdonald Tunnel takes westbound traffic at half the gradient of the Connaught Tunnel, which handles eastbound descending traffic. The inset map on the right shows the line before the Connaught Tunnel was built, crossing the Illecillewaet River three times and Loop Brook twice, on five progressively higher trestle bridges (one was 1000 feet long by 200 feet high), and traversing the treacherous face of Mount Abbot. The west portal of the Connaught Tunnel is 540 feet lower than the maximum height reached by the original track in Rogers Pass. Two hundred lives were lost to avalanches in this area between 1886 and 1911.

This group went to great lengths to comply with its instructions, which were that if at all possible the CPR should retain sole occupation of Rogers Pass. They finally decided that the railway had to move over and accept company.

A total of five alternative routes were looked at, including one through Moberly Pass and one through Jumbo Pass, sixty miles south of Golden (see the map "Six Routes Across the Selkirks"). The engineers found that a route sharing Rogers Pass with the railway was by far the best alternative. To build this to TCH standards was estimated to cost $28 million, whereas to improve the big bend route, two and a quarter times as long, to the same standards would take $31 million.

A few comments about Jumbo Pass, the odd man in the group, are appropriate. A road on this route was a long-lasting dream of the residents of both East and West Kootenays as a shortcut between their regions. It was especially coveted later on by ski enthusiasts on either side of the Selkirks wishing to more easily reach the other's ski slopes, or maybe to establish even better ones, and of course it was strongly supported by all the local Chambers of Commerce.

This view, south of Jumbo Pass beyond Kootenay Lake, shows the type of terrain surveyors had to deal with.

The darker road surface shown above on the Big Bend Highway is probably oil to lay the dust. It did not last long in the hot summers of the upper Columbia. The only saving grace was the lack of traffic, as most travellers to or from the east went by the southern route to avoid the long detour. The Columbia is in the background. As it appears to be flowing towards the viewer, the car must be bound from Golden to Boat Encampment on the highway's eastern leg, and the mountains shown are the Selkirks.

Jumbo Pass should have been called Jumbo Ridge, as it is actually a narrow hogback, 7500 feet in elevation, located between two flanking mountains in the 11,000-foot range, Jumbo Mountain and Mount Earl Grey. To use this route for a road, a two-mile tunnel with portal elevations around 5500 feet above sea level would need to be built. Even the combined enthusiasm of every Chamber of Commerce in the area could not persuade the Department of Highways to take this on. (In its examination of Jumbo Pass, the group of highway engineers was probably not aware of a tiny chapter in B.C.'s transportation history that put them in the footsteps of pioneer cattle drovers. In 1892, cattle were driven from Toby Creek near Invermere, over Jumbo Pass, and down to Kootenay Lake where they were shipped by boat to feed the miners at Riondel.)

The outcome of the study was the choice of Rogers Pass over any idea to improve the Big Bend Highway to Trans-Canada standards. No doubt the railway would have preferred the latter, but it seemed the CPR's influence had finally waned by the 1950s. The advantage to the local economy, and to the province, that would be realized in shorter travel times and lower vehicle operating costs played a large part in this decision. As well, there was a feeling it was Columbia River hydro-electric potential, not anything the road men could do, that swung the pendulum in the mountains of British Columbia away from the railway.

This study gained the immediate approval of the Trans-Canada Highway Division of the federal government, and as already mentioned, the engineer who submitted it impressed Ottawa so much that the government requested his services on loan to work on its share of the highway.

The steeper grades acceptable to roadbuilding made it possible to hold to the northern slope of the Illecillewaet River valley and Bear Creek valley, so roadbuilders were able to avoid the avalanche-prone mountainside across from it. (The railway had solved its avalanche problems by building the Connaught Tunnel.) The highway was completed in 1962 and British Columbia had an emerging, and soon to be exceptional, Interior road system—no thanks at all to the railways. The route has given safe service year-round ever since and will do so in the future, provided that adequate measures are taken against avalanches.

In the report leading to the choice of route, these highway engineers concluded that the overall costs per mile of the Rogers Pass roadway were similar to those of the Fraser Canyon work.

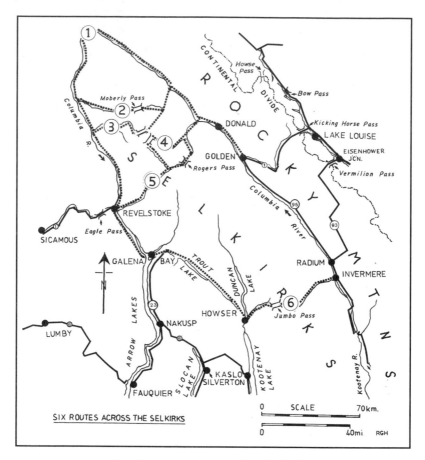

Six Routes Across the Selkirks

From the Top

1. *The Big Bend Route, Revelstoke to Golden, is approximately 180 miles.*
2. *Goldstream River to Gold River by Moberly Pass and a two-mile tunnel.*
3. *By Downie and Sorcerer Creek to Batchelor Creek and a 5000-foot summit.*
4. *Illecillewaet River to Tangier Creek and then over a 6500-foot summit to Mountain Creek.*
5. *The Rogers Pass Route, Revelstoke to Donald, is 76 miles.*
6. *The Jumbo Pass Route from Revelstoke to Eisenhower Junction, the eastern terminus of Highway 93, is 234 miles as against 158 miles by Rogers Pass.*

Using these criteria it is possible to estimate what the cost of the Rogers Pass route would have been in 1927, the year that the canyon road was completed. That construction cost $25,000 per mile approximately, so the 90 miles of Rogers Pass would have come in at $2.25 million. The Canada Parks estimate for its section of the big bend route was $11,000 per mile in the same year, for a total cost of $2.16 million. Obviously extra cost was not a factor in the decision to deny British Columbia the Rogers Pass in 1929.

Ironically the worst part of the Trans-Canada Highway in British Columbia as this is written is the section immediately east of Golden where the highway passes through the lower canyon of the Kicking Horse River. With present traffic flows in summer it is more accident-prone than any other part of the highway; it is also more difficult to widen due to the extreme steepness of the slopes and the instability of the broken rock, clays, and silts.

As for the railway through the Rockies, after employing 10,000 men for two years and spending tens of millions of dollars in 1909, the CPR eliminated the horrendous 4.5 percent grade on the four-mile "big hill" by means of the spiral tunnels and was adding tunnels to the line in the lower Kicking Horse Canyon for many years after that. In the Selkirks the railway decided in the 1980s that the grades originally included in the Rogers Pass section should be lessened in the westbound direction as part of a twin-tracking of the line. This was to better accommodate the unit coal trains hauling from the East Kootenay coalfields to Roberts Bank south of Vancouver. These trains came up the Kootenay-Columbia line to Golden, then on to Revelstoke and Mission by the mainline. To twin-track through Rogers Pass the CPR built a second tunnel, the Mount Macdonald Tunnel, twice the length and half the gradient of the Connaught.[22]

A.B. Rogers left a legacy of trouble for his railway peers and for those following him by rail and road; a legacy that would simply not have existed had he gone by Howse Pass.

Parks Canada is responsible for snow removal in national parks, including Rogers and Kicking Horse Passes. The piece of artillery displayed here is the property of the Canadian Army, which fires it. The avalanche zones affecting provincial highways are denied such national armament. There, less powerful commercial avalaunchers are used. Their sole advantage is that misfires degrade relatively fast. If the howitzer shells used by the army fail to detonate, they do not degrade quickly. Misfired shells have been found in highway ditches after spring thaw. The lower picture shows some of the modern snowsheds in Rogers Pass.

Section Two

British Columbia's Southern Interior From Crowsnest Pass to Hope

Chapter 5

Hope to Princeton

*A competition for routes through
the mountains leaves no winners*

In British Columbia's transportation history Allison Pass has been handed the part of a marriageable maiden living far off in the Cascade Mountains near the American border, waiting for her lover to arrive. The potential bridegroom was the Coast to Kootenay road connection, commonly known today as the Hope-Princeton Highway. The courtship was to be a lengthy one.

John Fall Allison, a young prospector from the eastern seaboard, first discovered the pass in 1860. Impressing Governor James Douglas soon after his arrival in Victoria, he was assigned the task of exploring the mountains east of Hope.[1]

The consummation of the love affair, the date when road and pass were eternally joined, did not take place until 90 years later. It was the longest delay in the joining of a transportation need to its solution in the history of the province. Frustrations of the good people of the border towns east of Hope reached a peak in the late 1930s when this road project became widely known as "the great procrastination."[2]

Standing in the way of this delightful union like wary parents on watch were the Skagit Bluffs, located some 30 miles east of

Shown here at the homestead in Princeton is Susan, the hardy pioneer wife of John Allison, and six of the fourteen children she bore him, one dying at birth. She withstood a fire brought by the nearby forest and a flood brought by the Similkameen and rebuilding made necessary by both. She finally put it all down on paper in a book edited by Margaret Ormsby. She was truly a founding mother of British Columbia.

John Fall Allison (1825-1897) was born in England, emigrated to America at age 12, and was a California gold-rush miner at 25. He became a B.C. pioneer trailbuilder at age 35.

Hope, a barrier that was considered difficult but not impossible to overcome. By 1909 all parties seemed in agreement, the marriage would have proceeded, and the road would have been built then and there had not Thomas Shaughnessy, president of the Canadian Pacific Railway, and James Jerome Hill, president of an American railway, the Great Northern, come upon the scene. To tell this story properly it is necessary to go back to the heady days of the building of Canada's first transcontinental railway.

When Jim Hill resigned from the board of directors of the CPR in 1883 and sold all the stock owned by himself and his Dutch-American backers in New York State, he did not do so in a calm and placid frame of mind. Far from it—he did it in a rage at the treason of William Cornelius Van Horne, the American whom he had brought in as general manager of the railway specifically to ensure that the planned transcontinental line would detour south

American William Cornelius Van Horne (left) was fully as stubborn and determined as Canadian Jim Hill, and his great service to Canada stands firm, as does the railway he built—and as the railway Hill built does for the United States. Van Horne agonized over whether or not to build through Rogers Pass or to go around the big bend of the Columbia. He chose the former and for the rest of his life he had to live with the disasters and loss of life that followed in the years before the Connaught Tunnel was opened. He also went ahead with the line through Kicking Horse Pass amid controversy. It was all forgiven in the immensity of the achievement of a railway across Canada.

James Jerome Hill (right) was a man of monumental determination and ability. He was a driving force in the Canadian Pacific Railway until his and William Cornelius Van Horne's paths diverged and he left. While there, he decided the course of the CPR line through the Prairies and across the Rockies. He then extended his Minnesota-based railway to become an American transcontinental line, renamed the Great Northern. Were it not for his death in 1916, the GN would have left a much larger footprint in British Columbia. The loss of an eye early in life did little for his appearance (until he got a good glass one), but his railway was beautiful. His proud boast was that he had never received a cent of public funds for it. No president of a Canadian railway could make that statement. Also beautiful was the company logo, depicting a mountain goat and the Rocky Mountains.

of Lake Superior through the state of Minnesota, which was the centre of Hill's major enterprises in rail and steamboat transportation at that time.[3] Hill was a man of rather close horizons, but also a man of wide ability.

Van Horne the American had become much more Canadian in spirit than Hill the Canadian had ever been, and he had enthusiastically supported locating the entire railway, including the section north of Lake Superior, in Canada, which was quite contrary to his sponsor's wishes. When this alignment gained the consent of the board of directors, Hill had nowhere to go but out the door, and he took his financial backing with him. He swore then that the frustration and harassment of the CPR, particularly along the international border, would be the highest priority in all of his future endeavours—his actual words were, "Even if I have to go to Hell for it, and shovel coal!"[4]

Jim Hill was resourceful, and after leaving the CPR he extended the scope of his Minnesota railway across the continent. He was at the helm of the Great Northern (GN), today the Burlington Northern, when it completed its transcontinental line in 1893. This was the second nationwide American railway aimed at Puget Sound, and it was the closest to Canada.

Fortunately for Hill, mineral wealth was discovered in the Kootenays just north of him at the same time as he was looking for business in the western United States and Canada. This happened coincidentally with British Columbians realizing that they were dealing with a CPR monopoly—and the best way to deal with a monopoly is to invite competition.

Notwithstanding his success with railways, Hill was still a steamboat man at heart, having started with a sternwheeler on the Red River before he branched out into iron horses. And despite the loss of one eye when he was a child in Canada, he could see very clearly how to capture the transportation contracts to haul high-grade minerals recently discovered near Sandon, B.C. The mines were only a short trip over the mountains from Kaslo, which was on Kootenay Lake, and the easy way to Kootenay Lake for

The Nelson *was launched in 1891 and was the pioneer sternwheeler on Kootenay Lake. J.J. Hill of the Great Northern Railway hired it in 1893 to haul ore barges from Kaslo to the head of the lake and upriver over the border to Bonners Ferry, Idaho, a point on his mainline. This was his first move in the harassment of the CPR. CP replied by purchasing the Columbia and Kootenay Steam Navigation Company, the owners of the* Nelson, *and denying its use to him. Hill then acquired his own sternwheelers, and a bitter fight for supremacy of the waters followed— one of the few battles that Jim Hill ever lost. The* Nelson's *engine and some of its machinery came from the* Skuzzy *via the* Skuzzy II. *Machinery circulated around in those days. The engine was a very powerful one, which was one reason the* Skuzzy *made it through Hells Gate and also why the* Nelson *could tow heavy barges against the current on the Kootenay River.*

Jim Hill was by the Kootenay River, which flowed past Bonners Ferry, Idaho, a stop on the mainline of his new GN Railway. (See map "Railways of Southern British Columbia.")

Helped by an associate in British Columbia who obtained a charter for a narrow-gauge railway from Sandon to Kaslo, Hill laid his plans. Before the CPR even knew what he was up to, he'd started laying narrow-gauge trackage over the mountains to Kaslo— albeit with very steep grades. From Kaslo the haul was south by water. The ore barges and the sternwheeler to push them were provided by the Columbia & Kootenay Steam Navigation Company (C&KSN), using the *Nelson*, which had been launched in that town in 1891. Hill eventually purchased a spur line from

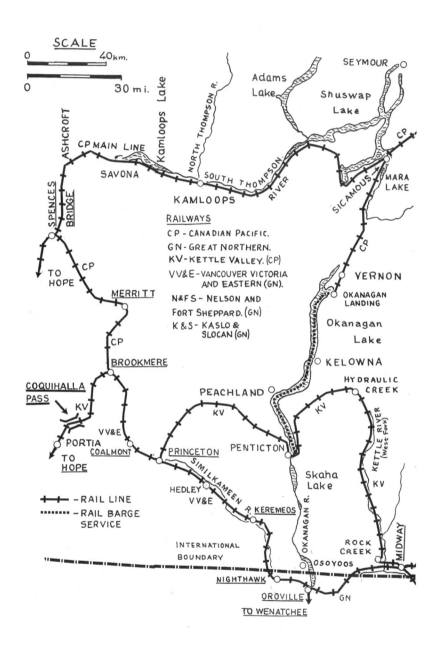

Railways of Southern British Columbia, 1885–1916

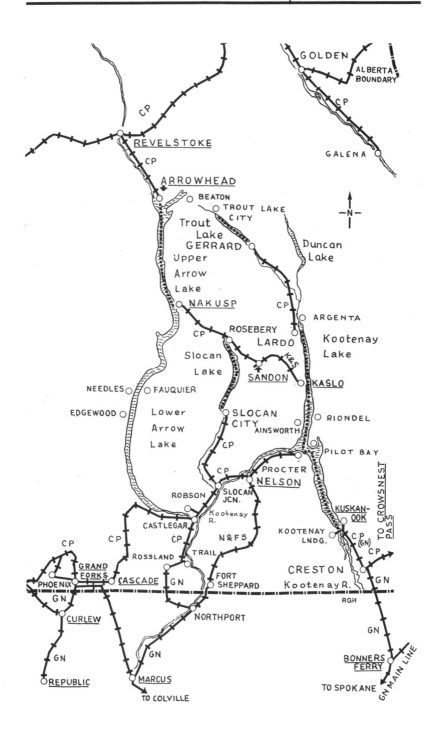

Bonners Ferry to the south end of Kootenay Lake to reduce the barge haul; it reached the bottom of the lake on the east shore at a village called Kuskanook and was of standard gauge.[5]

This was only the first step in James Hill's harassment of Van Horne and the CPR, and it turned out very well for British Columbians. In 1896 the CPR started laying rail from Lethbridge westwards through Crowsnest Pass, executing an expansion plan that might not have existed without Hill to urge it on. Of course the Canadian taxpayer abetted the process in the form of CPR's Crowsnest Agreement with the dominion government. This agreement became one of the most controversial pieces of railway legislation in Canada's history.[6]

Once the CPR had arranged the subsidy with government, which was $11,000 per mile for 250 miles, the company's managers did not hesitate. They hired Andrew Onderdonk's capable ramrod Michael Haney. He assembled 5000 men and 2000 teams of horses, and in November 1898 they arrived at Kootenay Landing at the south end of Kootenay Lake, having built the full distance from twelve miles east of Crowsnest Pass in slightly under 24 months.[7] It was not done without filling the wards of St. Eugene Hospital in Cranbrook with typhoid patients from unhygienic camps or, later on, filling the same wards with railwaymen hurt in gumbo slides from the clay banks hastily cut out of the hillsides on either side of that townsite.[8] Some of these clays had a tendency, when wet, to take up their own "angle of repose," which was usually much flatter than that of normal railway grade excavation.

In 1896 the CPR bought out the C&KSN, which in turn forced Hill to regroup and find new water transport. The Kootenay transportation war was on.[9] This war came to actual blows, man to man, in Sandon. Instead of swinging spike hammers they swung cudgels. The fight was over land that the GN claimed but on which the CPR built a depot. As always, Jim Hill was the general but in the wings. He brought in an assault force, prisoners were taken (temporarily), and the CPR's brand new station was hooked up to a locomotive and pulled to oblivion. Jim Hill denied everything,

This study of a railway versus gravity was taken on the Kaslo to Sandon line. When the GN suspended service and began to lift tracks, Premier McBride arranged its sale to a local syndicate. The CPR finally took over the section from the summit to Kaslo and widened it from narrow guage to standard. The photo was taken at Payne Bluff. The line ran through high passses subject to heavy snowfall and it was often closed for weeks in the spring due to heavy snow slides.

That conductor had better not sneeze, or he's dead!

but he certainly came out of this battle ahead. Barrie Sanford describes it very well in *McCulloch's Wonder*.

The CPR continued to look west, and in 1898 it purchased the Columbia and Western Railway and its charter, as well as the Trail smelter, from August Heinze. Presumably inspired by these infusions, the men of Montreal went on to achieve the almost incredible feat of building 100 miles of track through the Monashee Mountains in one year. In September 1899 they celebrated the arrival of their first train into Grand Forks from Medicine Hat, Alberta. The CPR never received the recognition it deserved for building the southern B.C. line, which crossed the Rockies and the Purcell, Selkirk, and Monashee Mountains: a truly remarkable feat.[10]

A sidelight to this, and one of interest to highway historians, is the wagon trail the CPR built between Castlegar and Cascade to move supplies and equipment westwards to support construction. Information on the location of this trail and its eventual fate is missing; it apparently vanished after the railway construction. It crossed an area that gave road access problems for many years, and it does not seem to have been used by the road authority. After they reached Cascade, the CPR surveyors carried on with a preliminary reconnaissance westward, finally traversing the Coquihalla summit and reaching Hope in January 1900.[11]

In 1901, again working through his agents in B.C., Hill acquired the controlling interest in the Vancouver, Victoria and Eastern Railway (VV&E), and the race to the coast began. Hill built another connection into British Columbia from his mainline, this one to Cascade and on to Grand Forks. Then his border-hopping railway went into the States and back into Canada again at Midway, B.C., competing fiercely for mine haul wherever it was available. In 1904 he announced that he intended to build from Curlew through Oroville and Nighthawk in Washington, then back into B.C. to Princeton, Hope, and eventually Vancouver. The map "Railways of Southern British Columbia" shows the routes of the VV&E, the line in British Columbia that Hill financed and controlled, and one that brought with it that vital charter for a coast railway. The building of the VV&E from Princeton up the Tulameen River valley to Coalmont in 1909 to 1913 had a great deal to do with the Hope-Princeton Highway's jilting of Allison Pass in 1909, and the twisting path to that breach began nearly a decade earlier.

That path began in 1901 in Victoria, where James Dunsmuir was premier. The people of British Columbia had become even more upset about the CPR monopoly, but they were also getting a bit concerned about the activities of these vigorous Americans. Premier Dunsmuir did not know which way to jump for a while, although he eventually came down for the CPR. While testing the wind, Dunsmuir acted like a true politician and took a step that he thought would please everyone. He authorized a survey and study of the Cascade Mountains between Hope and Princeton to find the best route for a railway and to estimate costs, and he chose 66-year-old Edgar Dewdney for the job.

Edgar Dewdney was the legendary trailbuilder of colonial days in B.C. The Dewdney Trail, which ran from Hope to a point close to Cranbrook along B.C.'s southern boundary, was named for him. He also mapped a route to the Omineca gold rush and located the trail to Hazelton in northern B.C. Dewdney had completed a term as Lieutenant-Governor of B.C. some three years before this and was in retirement, but nonetheless he took on the survey.[12]

This decision seemed logical and proper at the time, but it turned out to be one of a series of choices and events that proved disastrous for the development of transportation in southern British Columbia for the next 30 years. Among other adverse factors were the boom or bust economy, the Great War, and, of course, politics. The appointment of Edgar Dewdney to survey the Cascade Mountains was a wrong decision because though Dewdney was an excellent surveyor, fully experienced in trail and wagon road building in these mountains, he had no experience in the design and maintenance of railways in mountainous terrain. The only engineers with that experience in Canada worked for the CPR, and at that time they had their hands full with the problems brought on by excessive snowfalls in Rogers Pass. The other source of expertise was of course the Great Northern Railway and its engineering staff, especially a man called John Stevens, of whom more later.

The problem was that Premier Dunsmuir could not use either of these resources because he was acting politically to placate both organizations, as well as the public. To choose a man from one side would have alienated the other. Edgar Dewdney, who was neutral, seemed to be the perfect choice, but he was not.

In any event, the survey commenced in August 1901. Dewdney had a man named Henry Carry on his crew, along with Walter Moberly's brother Frank. Carry was an excellent surveyor and did a very good job. This was noted and he was subsequently hired by the CPR. Dewdney completed the survey by mid-October and came up with three alternatives, which are shown in the map "Dewdney's Three Routes."[13]

One was by the Coquihalla Pass, more or less on the line the Kettle Valley Railway took some ten years later. The second followed the Coquihalla River from Hope to an unnamed stream

The Honourable Edgar Dewdney (1835-1916), the foremost surveyor and builder of trails in British Columbia's colonial days, became the Lieutenant-Governor of the province in 1892 and served in that capacity until 1897. Elected to the Legislative Council in 1868 and 1870, he partook in the confederation debate and became an M.P. in 1874, serving for many years in the Canadian House of Commons. He was Indian Commissioner for Manitoba and the North-West Territories and Lieutenant-Governor of the latter.

The background photo shows Dewdney's trail at Skagit Bluffs, a section that was in use until after World War II. This is somewhat lower than the present highway.

TRAILS INTO THE PAST

When Edgar Dewdney strode up the trail from Hope into the Cascade Mountains in 1901 to identify possible railway routes to Princeton, his mind must have been full of memories. The trail had two arms, one bound for Nicola and the other for the Similkameen, and they were the only means of travel through these mountains.

Most of the Hope-Similkameen trail to Princeton had been built by Dewdney himself, under the supervision of Sergeant McColl of the Royal Engineers 41 years before. As Dewdney went farther east along the Similkameen River, he joined the old Hudson's Bay route that had been improved by John Allison who had discovered Allison Pass.

Allison had died in 1897, but his wife and a number of his thirteen children still lived in Princeton. Most certainly Dewdney would have visited them. Susan Allison was his sister-in-law.

Susan and her sister Jane had been abandoned by their father, who left his wife and children four years after the family had arrived in Fort Hope in 1860. Thomas Glennie left only the house he built, a rather pretentious log structure, located on the brigade trail a few miles east of the fort. His attempts at farming had been about as poor as his handle on life, and all that he could do when his money ran out was to leave Hope and family behind. Fortunately the kind people in Fort Hope at that time included George and Marie Landvoigt, who owned the general store. They befriended the beleaguered Glennies and Marie even gave Mrs. Glennie her schoolteacher job.

George Landvoigt also would have come at once to Dewdney's mind. It was Landvoigt who had most to do with the building of the Hope-Nicola trail through Coquihalla Pass, completed in 1876, two years before his accidental death. Landvoigt was B.C.'s first road superintendent at Hope. He was also the justice of the peace, a trail outfitter, and he ran a sawmill. The Hope-Nicola trail was his masterpiece. A full six feet in width, it was greatly superior to the Hope-Similkameen trail, but it soon fell into disuse when the Canadian Pacific Railway arrived in 1886. It was totally destroyed by the Kettle Valley Railway 30 years later.

One of the rail route alternatives considered by Dewdney was a line using Allison Pass. Colonel Richard Moody had first recognized this as a possibility when he received a description of the pass from John Allison in 1860. Dewdney knew Moody too, and was aware of his thoughts on the pass.

east of where Boston Bar Creek meets the Coquihalla. Christening it Carry Creek, they determined that it descended steeply from a 4500-foot-high summit to the east. They also found that a stream flowed eastward from this same summit. The surveyors named this Railroad Creek and noted that it flowed into the Tulameen from Railroad Pass at a much gentler pace than Carry Creek ran west. Railroad Creek runs into the Columbia watershed (see map "Rail Routes by the Tulameen and Coquihalla"). The third route was by Allison Pass, as the highway goes now.

The Railroad Pass route had an advantage in length but a distinct disadvantage in slope of land as Carry Creek drops about 2000 feet in five miles, about four times steeper than the allowable grade for a railway. In order to build the line with a gradient acceptable for rail use it was necessary to extend the line into the upper canyon of the Coquihalla River and run upstream on the eastern slope for about eight miles. This line would run along a very precipitous

Dewdney's Three Routes
for a Railway Through the Cascades

The Way They Went. *Through Coquihalla Pass—which led to the abandonment of the line in a few decades due to instability in the slopes of the Upper Coquihalla Canyon.*

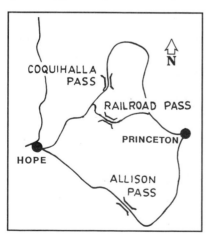

The Way They Should Have Gone. *Through Railroad Pass with a tunnel. Jim Hill called for tenders to build this tunnel but was dissuaded by a rift with his son, which spread to the GN board of directors.*

The Way the CPR Thought They Might Have to Go. *Through Allison Pass—and indecision about this halted the building of a road through the pass at a crucial time. This led to a 25-year delay in using this pass for a highway.*

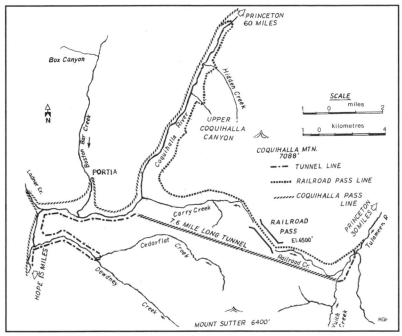

Rail Routes by the Tulameen and Coquihalla

All lines, except that shown by Coquihalla Pass, are derived from specu-
lation, with the assistance of modern contour mapping from aerial
photography, including that for the Coquihalla Highway.

mountainside and the northwestern exposure would mean it was
subject to avalanches and snowslides.

All these problems could have been avoided by driving a tunnel
under the high ground near Railroad Pass. Such a tunnel would go
under the pass, as the Connaught Tunnel did at Rogers Pass. The
Railroad Pass tunnel, 50 percent longer than the Connaught, would
have saved 30 miles over the line through Coquihalla Pass as finally
built: 62 miles from Hope to Princeton as against 92. It would
also have lessened the grades on the route. Jim Hill made both of
these points when he called for tenders on the tunnel in 1909. (See
"Rail Routes by the Tulameen and Coquihalla.")

Coquihalla Pass differed from Railroad Pass in that it could be
reached from either direction by easy gradients, using the Coldwater
and Coquihalla valleys. However, the latter had serious instability

problems in the upper canyon close to the pass. These and Hill's proposed tunnel will be described in detail later.

The final alternative Dewdney considered was via Allison Pass, which was longer by at least ten miles and was always regarded as a last resort, although Colonel Moody of the Royal Engineers had cited it as a possible rail location.[14] Allison Pass is 4469 feet above sea level and has considerably less snowfall than Coquihalla Pass, a fact mentioned by Dewdney.

In 1902 Dewdney submitted two alternatives: Coquihalla Pass and Railroad Pass. He did not consider a tunnel. The Railroad Pass line, at 4500 feet, fell out of favour due to its height of land as opposed to the Coquihalla Pass at 3646 feet, but it would have saved much mileage in the trip from Hope to Princeton.

A few years later, Edgar Dewdney stated that he never liked any of these routes through the Cascade Mountains because of the engineering difficulties inherent in all of them. He said that in his opinion the best solution would have been to use the Fraser Canyon, with a line from Spences Bridge to Merritt and down to Princeton as the final link in the Coast to Kootenay railway. Subsequent events proved that there was much wisdom in this.[15]

The only result of Dewdney's survey seemed to be the GN's consideration of a tunnel under Railroad Pass, which was never built. The CPR and the VV&E continued planning their coast-to-Kootenay lines, though construction was slowed by economic depression. In 1905 the GN/VV&E received permission from Prime Minister Wilfrid Laurier for an international border crossing so they could build from Midway to Princeton. CPR men blocked the line, claiming their company owned a tiny piece of land near Midway that the VV&E was planning to build over. A pitched battle ensued, ended by expropriation of the land for the VV&E.

In 1909 the CPR bought the Kettle Valley Railway, with its charter to build to the coast from Midway, and hired Andrew McCulloch to push the line through. In 1910 CPR men, in their guise as employees of the Kettle Valley Railway, had not yet left Midway with any rail grade but were surveying ahead through the

LAURIER'S LAPSE

Canadian Prime Minister Sir Wilfrid Laurier's seemingly unconditional permission to J.J. Hill, president of the Great Northern Railway, to enter Canada at Nighthawk en route to Hope and Vancouver in 1905 has to be viewed as a grave disservice to Canadian interests.

That was the year when the GN and the CPR (through its subsidiary the Kettle Valley Railway) were engaged in a rather foolish contest to be the first to the coast. Both survey crews knew that a well-known Canadian engineer had judged it would be extremely difficult to find one acceptable rail route in the area, let alone two. Jim Hill had exercised great pressure on Canadians; it was time that he got some back. Who better to apply this than the Prime Minister? A strong but reasonable condition of entry was all that was needed. Laurier could have insisted that the Americans agree to grant running rights to Canadian railways on any through trackage the GN built between Nighthawk and Hope. This would be a reciprocal proviso on a share-the-cost basis.

Had such a condition been extended, several things might have happened. Jim Hill might have stayed away altogether—not a bad result for Canada. Had he built anyway, the KVR might have used the proviso to share a line up the gentle grade of the Similkameen valley with the Americans. This would have been infinitely better than climbing 2570 feet to the Osprey Lake Summit.

The map entitled "A Much Easier Way from Penticton to Princeton" shows that if the two railways had shared track, the Kettle Valley line could have run from Penticton south past Skaha Lake, over a low summit near Yellow Lake to Keremeos (the route Highway 3A takes today). The KVR could have joined the GN at Keremeos and used its line to Princeton up the Similkameen valley, rather than running northwest out of Penticton over the Osprey Lake Summit.

Such enforced co-operation might well have been extended to the Railroad Pass Tunnel, with both parties sharing the cost of that, a much better result for British Columbia. A line through Coquihalla Pass could never have competed with one through a tunnel.

But Laurier's policy, one reason for his defeat at the polls, was full reciprocity with the United States, and he had alienated himself from the CPR board of directors by his support of the Grand Trunk Railway. These factors probably contributed to his lapse.

Coquihalla Pass to Hope. However, they did not realize that in 1909 Hill had filed plans with the Board of Railway Commissioners in Ottawa for a line through Coquihalla Pass. When his idea of running a tunnel through Railroad Pass fell apart, Hill returned to Coquihalla Pass and even obtained a court injunction to keep the KVR men from interfering with his survey through that pass.[16]

The Great Northern was already driving a short tunnel through intervening high ground on the outskirts of Princeton in order to get a good grade up the Tulameen valley on the way to Coalmont, and the GN rail grade was under construction up that valley with a great burst of activity in which the river was bridged three times. It was obvious to any observer that there was no way that valley could accommodate more than one railway, so Jim Hill had thrown up a very substantial barrier to the CPR's using Railroad Pass instead of the Coquihalla. That left Allison Pass as the only CPR alternative.[17]

The scene now shifts back to Victoria and to 1909, which was a very significant twelve-month period in the transportation history of the province. This was the year when Richard McBride, premier from 1903 to 1915, called an election and announced that he was approving a second railway through the Fraser Canyon (see Chapter 3). Two of his ministers resigned, but he went ahead anyway.[18] As previously related, he told his Minister of Public Works to drop any ideas he had about replacing the road through the Fraser Canyon and to find some other way for the travelling public, in the newfangled contraptions called automobiles, to wend its way from the lower mainland to the Interior.[19]

"Good Roads" Taylor immediately started planning for a road from Hope to Princeton. There would be a new road from Princeton northwards to Merritt and then on to Kamloops, with a cutoff to Ashcroft for Cariboo traffic. The new way through the Cascade Mountains would also connect eastwards to Keremeos and points beyond.

Taylor assigned a consulting engineer by the name of A.E. Cleveland from Vancouver to locate the new road, and after the 1910 surveying season was over an announcement was made that

From Canadian Pacific's archives comes this picture of a Kettle Valley train doubleheaded by engines 5127 and 5207. This particular train included a car with roof vents that accommodated fresh fruit.

Midway CPR station (inset) was located in the midst of a rare area of flat land amidst the southern B.C. mountains. It is now a museum, as it is an historic place. Midway was as far as the CPR got with their southern British Columbia line from Crowsnest Pass in January of 1900. From there on the Okanagan Highlands were a barrier, and ten years would pass before the Kettle Valley Railway was organized to follow the valley of its name westward. It is not clear whether Midway was so named because it was halfway along the Dewdney Trail between Hope and Kingsgate, or midway between the Rockies and the Pacific Ocean. It is both.

it would go by Silverhope Creek and Gibson Pass. This came as a surprise to many people who knew the country, and it immediately raised the red flag on a hidden agenda. To start with, this route bypassed Hope as it turned off a few miles west of the town. It was at least eight miles longer than the Skagit Bluffs-Allison Pass route and it ignored 29 miles of wagon road already built that only required widening.[20]

By contrast, the rough trail through the Silverhope valley had a reputation for washouts and snowslides as it was at the foot of formidable mountain peaks joined together by high ridges, all facing west and first in line to intercept the precipitation-laden storms from the Pacific Ocean, which move inland through the lower Fraser Valley. These peaks of the Skagit Range contain the only glaciation still in existence in the Canadian Cascades. Despite these adverse features, the route was approved. About ten miles of rough-ed-out roadway were built at the west end and fourteen miles at the east end by 1914, after which World War I closed down all work. It did not start up again after the war, and Gibson Pass was never again considered for a highway.[21]

The question of course is, why did they not locate the road through Allison Pass? An assessment of Premier McBride's political position as a result of recent railway decisions is needed to answer this question. The good premier was in deep trouble with many people over his support for a second transcontinental railway in the southern half of the province, and not only with the two cabinet members whom he had lost over it. His growing list of adversaries now included the top men of the CPR who were furious with him. A second railway through the Fraser Canyon would destroy their monopoly. McBride had to do something quickly to get back into the CPR's good graces, a very practical position for any premier of British Columbia. To achieve this he announced that his government was supporting the CPR's Kettle Valley Railway as the Coast-to-Kootenay link, and he also promised $5000 per mile for over 100 miles of it from the public purse.[22] This $5 million dollar pacifier did the trick for McBride but not the road authority.

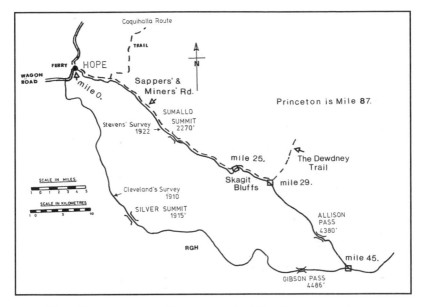

Two Routes from Hope to the Similkameen River

A.E. *Cleveland's 1910 survey parallels Silverhope Creek over Silver Summit, then follows Klesilkwa, Skagit, and Nepopekum Creek valleys to Gibson Pass, and over that divide to the Columbia watershed. Nepopekum Creek is winding, steep sided, and fast rising. It is unused for trail or road to this day. From Gibson Pass the survey follows Little Muddy Creek to the Similkameen River.*

In 1922 H.S. Stevens, a DPW employee, surveyed a line along the Dewdney Trail past Skagit Bluffs, leaving that trail at Mile 29 to follow the Skagit River to Allison Pass and eastwards to join Cleveland's line. From Mile 54 Stevens followed the benches west of the Similkameen over Sunday Summit. Cleveland descended into the Similkameen canyon and followed that to Princeton. Stevens' 87-mile line is that of today's highway.

A press release found in Department of Public Works files, dated July 11, 1913, describes the Gibson Pass route as part of a Pacific Highway development running from Blaine, Washington, via the Cariboo to Alaska. Promotion of this highway was a tourism development device in the western United States in the early 1900s ("Follow the Pacific Northwards!"), but the concept never caught on in B.C. The press release writer seems apologetic about the route and describes meadowlands and mineral resources along it that simply were not there. The goal was obviously to justify the Gibson Pass route. A copy of "The Pacific Highway" is in Appendix I.

When the Hope-Princeton road link was announced, the CPR was also plagued with a problem named Jim Hill. At that moment Allison Pass was vital to the railway. It was not so hard sharing Allison Pass with a road, but the prospect of building through Skagit Bluffs alongside a road held no appeal whatsoever. That section of high-backed cliffs was a substantial barrier. The road could go anywhere but there, stated the CPR. When Premier McBride announced his support for the railway, Thomas Shaughnessy no doubt requested that he order his road surveyors to find another way to Princeton other than by Skagit Bluffs. The premier probably instructed Thomas Taylor accordingly, and the Gibson Pass route was dressed up to look like a surveyor's choice. It is very difficult to find any other reason for the endorsement of this route.

The speculative theory advanced here, that the CPR considered Skagit Bluffs unsuitable for both road and rail to be built side by side and so asked that the road be located elsewhere, is of course just that: speculation. It is the most forgiving reason from an engineering viewpoint. Cleveland might quite honestly have preferred the Gibson Pass route to Allison Pass, despite the latter having 29 miles already half built and being eight miles shorter. Or perhaps he was apprehensive about the bluffs, but this seems unlikely in a province that in the previous half century had built both a road and a railway through the Fraser Canyon.

Of course Premier McBride may have told them to take the longer route and approach it tentatively, to bide time and give the proposed railway a clear field in which to prove itself economically without the competition of a road. If this was the strategy it certainly succeeded. That railway was not challenged by a road for almost 35 years.

The battle between the GN/VV&E and the CPR/KVR came to a stalemate in 1912 and 1913. When Hill abandoned the idea of building a tunnel in Railroad Pass, he returned to the Coquihalla Pass route, thinking that he had cleverly forestalled the CPR, but a second look at his proposed route proved that his alignment was

This view of Skagit Bluffs with the present highway indicates their height and steepness and demonstrates why early railbuilders may not have wanted the company of a road in this short section.

faulty. The story is that his application to have his line changed to the other side of the canyon was refused because by that time the KVR had filed there. He took it to court and the Canadian judge favoured the CPR, denying the VV&E access.[23]

However the KVR could not start out from Princeton to make use of its advantage because the VV&E had preceded it to the Tulameen Valley and there was not room for a second railway. In this the Americans had the upper hand, their only trump card left since Laurier's departure and the defeat of free trade at the polls. The VV&E sat down to negotiate with Andrew McCulloch, and an agreement was struck in April 1913. The VV&E granted the KVR running rights on its line from Princeton to Brookmere and received in return similar rights on the Kettle Valley's Brookmere to Hope section. KVR construction through Coquihalla Pass went ahead. At the same time, the GN completed a line from Wenatchee to Oroville, a final cementing of its extension into Canada.

When the construction of the Coquihalla section of the Kettle Valley Railway was undertaken by an American contractor between 1913 and 1916, the six-foot-wide Hope-Nicola cattle trail, the pride and joy of George Landvoigt, the first road superintendent at Hope, was used for access throughout. When the work was finished, very little of the historic trail remained. In these years roads and trails stood a very distant second to the railway business, either Canadian or American. Once again the road authority came out second best!

Now a diversion to an intriguing piece of provincial transportation history arising from actions by those south of the border. The map "Rail Routes by the Tulameen and Coquihalla" shows a tunnel as an alternative to the routes by Railroad or Coquihalla Passes. It is included because Jim Hill called for tenders for an eight-mile tunnel in this location in 1909. After he received the tenders, the amounts of which were not revealed, he announced that he had dropped the proposal because it would take too long to build, and he turned to the alternative through the Coquihalla Pass.[24]

The decision not to build the tunnel was a real tragedy because it was the answer to the problem of building a railway through a mountain pass that both parties knew would only accommodate one line due to its steepness, its instability, and its avalanches. This tunnel, and the Tulameen valley route to it, would have saved 30 miles in the trip from Hope to Princeton, and it would have led to a much safer and more easily maintainable operation, at much less cost, than that through the upper canyon of the Coquihalla. This wrong decision was made for the wrong reason: because of a rather childish race to build a railway from British Columbia's Interior to its lower coast.

The tunnel is mentioned variously as either 7 or 8 miles in length, so the length shown on the map, at 7.6 miles, falls suitably between these figures. It is remarkable that Jim Hill entertained the idea of building a tunnel of this length in the Cascade Mountains in 1909, considering the state of the art of tunnel building in North America at the time. He certainly did not conceive the idea himself, and the only man near him who would have been experienced enough or courageous enough to propose such an undertaking was his chief engineer, a man named John F. Stevens. (European railway engineers built progressively longer tunnels in the 25-year period ending in 1905, when the 12.5-mile Simplon Tunnel was completed. Had the GN or the CPR brought in some of this expertise and equipment, the Railroad Pass Tunnel would have been no problem, but the railwaymen in North America did not keep up with their European brethren in this. If the CPR had imported the skills and equipment of the Swiss engineers earlier, it could have completed the Connaught Tunnel by 1885.[25])

John Stevens had discovered Marias Pass through the Rockies for Hill in 1889. Very soon after that he found and developed Stevens Pass (named after him) through the Cascade Mountains in Washington territory. There Stevens built the Cascade Tunnel in time for the opening of the GN transcontinental line in 1893.[26] At 2.63 miles in length it was the longest tunnel in the United States when it was completed. (A new tunnel, 7.78 miles long, was opened at the same site in 1929 after three years of work. It was the longest in the U.S. at that time and it kept the distinction until the 1950s.[27])

John Stevens had a look at the Railroad Pass line and would likely have considered it unusable without a tunnel. He was very well aware of the added value of tunnelling to deal with heavy snowfall areas. He probably conceived the tunnel in 1903, though it was six years before it went to tender.

Insight into Stevens' personality is gained from David McCullough's book on the Panama Canal, *The Path Between the Seas*. McCullough reports that Stevens left Hill in 1903 in an atmosphere totally lacking in dissension. Hill always referred to

These two Canadian Pacific locomotives are all shined up for this 1886 photograph. It would have been much better if they had burned wood in their fireboxes and nowhere else, but these high, bell-mouthed smokestacks spread burning embers far and wide in the hot summer breezes of the first hectic years of operation. The sparks burned trees in the mountains and grass on the prairie, and not in small measure. The fires destroyed mountain vegetation needed for stability, and they deprived the desperate first settlers in the Palliser triangle of a small agricultural return from grazing, which, prior to the sugar beet crop, was all the area could provide. A CPR botanist had seen the Palliser area a few years previously in a rare climatic wet cycle, and he had mistakenly called it farming land.

Slope instability plagued the railway for years, and the spark fire hazard did not die down with the advent of coal. The instability on the steep slopes of the upper Coquihalla Canyon was a terminal illness for the Kettle Valley Railway.

Stevens as "the best railway engineer in the world," and he had promoted him to chief executive officer of the railway. Stevens left because he wished to restore engineering as the main part of his work, according to his later statements.[28]

He went to the Chicago, Rock Island & Pacific Railway as a vice-president, and shortly after that Hill pressed President Theodore Roosevelt to appoint him as chief engineer of the Panama Canal. This recommendation got him the job in June 1905. Stevens brought a workable solution to the colossal task of excavating the Culebra Cut: introducing the use of railway transportation to move the material. He gained widespread public acclaim and approval for the initial success of this. However in January 1907 he rather suddenly resigned before the work was over, which both puzzled and annoyed Roosevelt. Nonetheless he immediately accepted the resignation because of some unwise remarks in Stevens' letter. (One of them was that there were many jobs open to him in America that "he would prefer to that of the Presidency of the United States," and he also said that he could earn much more than the "wise lawmakers" were paying him. Not exactly tactful words to a president.)[29]

Some engineers retain good reputations not only for the work they do, but also for their ability to be elsewhere when difficulties arise. Stevens appears to have had this ability, as an examination of the circumstances surrounding his departure from the Panama Canal and his resignation from the Great Northern Railway shows. The Canal seemed to be in the clear when Stevens left, but the picture changed quite rapidly for his successor. The cutting seemed successful, but a bad rainy season demonstrated that the inherent instability at Culebra was not overcome by Stevens' work, and the phrase "The more you dig the more you have to dig" came into being. Stevens was well out of it.[30] He then went to the New Haven Railroad and after that he seemed to move quite often, still retaining his wonderful reputation. Finally he was appointed by President Woodrow Wilson to do a rehabilitation study of the Trans-Siberian Railway, which lasted for five years, following which he retired. He died in 1943 at the age of 90.[31]

In 1903, the year of Stevens' sudden resignation from the GN, the railway was fully into the effort to upstage the CPR, one of the largest railways in North America. In 1902 Hill had started service to Republic, a very active mining centre in Washington State that could only be reached by way of Canada due to intervening difficult terrain. Hill's incursion infuriated the Canadian railway. In 1904 Hill announced his intention was not only to serve Republic, but to use a point on that line, Curlew, as the starting point for a line back into Canada and eventually through the Canadian Cascades to Hope and Vancouver.[32] Curlew was on the Kettle River, and this river and the Similkameen further on were Hill's way west.

That same year Hill let a contract for a bridge over the Fraser River to New Westminster to bring his line into B.C. from Seattle. These were heady times in Jim Hill's empire. The question is, why did Stevens pull out in the midst of all of this?

First you must remember that when Edgar Dewdney announced the findings of his 1902 study of the Cascades and the three routes, Allison, Coquihalla, and Railroad Passes, he privately stated that he did not like any of them and to his mind the CPR should build from Midway to Princeton, from there north to Merritt and Spences Bridge, and use the Fraser Canyon as the way through the Cascades. Publicly he confined himself to the comment that the Hope Mountains could not be crossed without encountering serious engineering difficulties.

There is little doubt that after this announcement the first on the scene to study these serious engineering difficulties would be Stevens and his surveyors. Could it be that Stevens agreed with Dewdney but hesitated to convey this to Jim Hill because of the latter's continuing obsession to get the best of Van Horne, who was still at the top in the CPR? Did he foresee that the GN could lose heavily in this highly questionable venture, a prediction that came true after Hill's premature death in 1916? Or did he simply wish to depart from the scene due to the growing alienation between Hill and his son Louis, who was being groomed to take over the presidency as his father aged?

Stevens would have immediately dismissed the Railroad Pass non-tunnel alternative as quite impossible, and he might also have rejected the line through Coquihalla Pass as unworkable. He knew Hill would be loath to accept Allison Pass, as that route was so much longer. Did he then conceive the tunnel and prepare plans for it, then gracefully depart the scene before the going got too rough, as he did in Panama?

Nobody was better qualified than Stevens to envision an eight-mile tunnel in that location at that time, or for that matter to build it. He had finished a shorter one just a few miles south at Stevens Pass less than ten years before. The Railroad Pass tunnel would have been three times as long, but it would not have been overly difficult to build. A road built through the pass could have provided easy access to the west portal, and it would have been possible to access the tunnel at various points along its length and ventilate it with sloping shafts. There is little doubt that Stevens could have successfully driven that tunnel for Hill. Its benefit to B.C. would have been immense, and whether the GN or the CPR had ended up as the owner, it might well have led to the continued operation of the line to this day.

If Stevens did propose the tunnel and prepare plans for it before he left, Hill simply put them on the shelf until his project was further along. Then in 1909 he put it out to tender. As a second string to his bow, Hill filed plans with the Board of Railway Commissioners in Ottawa for a line through Coquihalla Pass. There is evidence that his survey for this was hastily prepared, as it turned out to be on the less favourable side of the canyon for both exposure and stability, an indication that Stevens might not have been involved.

In his book *The Kettle Valley and Its Railway*, author Hal Riegger speculates that the tunnel plan was dropped in 1909 when Jim Hill was faced with continuing opposition from his son Louis. The son had become president in 1907, but the father soon regretted this. Riegger feels that the son lacked the vision and drive of the father, and this was obvious when Louis dropped the entire British Columbia venture immediately after his father died.

In his final years, the grand old man supported Carl Gray as an alternative to his offspring as president. Gray strongly supported Hill's activities in Canada. When he turned away from the tunnel, Hill said that he would return and build it later, and he never moved from that position. Had he lived and installed Carl Gray as president of his railway, it is almost a certainty that there would be a tunnel from Railroad Creek to Dewdney Creek today. Like many great achievers Hill was a gambler, and his hole card was the tunnel, but he did not live to use it—he was actually drawing his cards to make his play when he died. Given the problems later encountered by the CPR in the upper Coquihalla Canyon, a competing GN line, protected from slides and snow and 30 miles shorter, would very soon have put the Canadian railway out of business between Brookmere and Hope. For Hill this would have been the ultimate CPR harassment. The old man had the heart of a lion; his son did not. (Hill, Senior, the capitalist, also had feelings for the common people. The day after the city of Fernie burned to the ground on August 1, 1908, the first person on the phone to Mayor W.W. Tuttle was J.J. Hill speaking from his Minneapolis office. Hill informed the mayor that he could immediately draw up to $5000 from Hill's personal account to help citizens in need.[33])

There is little doubt that had J.J. Hill lived on and prevailed, the Great Northern Railway would not have retreated but would have advanced to forge closer economic ties between the two countries. In this he had an ally and a friend in Sir Wilfrid Laurier, the Canadian prime minister, whose departure from office in 1911 was a severe blow.[34]

It is also intriguing to speculate whether Stevens would have agreed to include the Coquihalla Pass line as an alternative to the tunnel in 1908 had he been there. An experienced railroad engineer of Stevens' calibre would have foreseen serious landslide and snowslide problems because of the nature of the terrain in the up-per canyon, an area of extreme instability, and steered Hill away from that location. He might have persuaded Andrew McCulloch, the chief engineer of the KVR, to share equally in the construction of the tunnel. (In the early part of his career McCulloch worked as an axeman under Stevens in Stevens Pass.) The GN had already built a line to Brookmere, but if such harmony had been reached between the two companies as to allow them to co-operate in con-structing the railway, it would have been easy for the GN to hand that line over to the CPR to form part of a Princeton-Merritt-Spences Bridge line.

The best description of the terrain in the upper Coquihalla Canyon is in a Department of Lands and Works response to a petition from the settlers at Douglas Lake for a trail through the

Coquihalla Pass in 1874. The DPW reported that the trailbuilders would have to traverse "miles of precipices with immense fragments of granite lying at the foot of them."[35] While the word immense is rather excessive, the rest of the phrase is an excellent description of weathered rock faces with scree or talus continually sliding off them, the prevailing condition in the canyon and one that contributed greatly to the demise of the KVR line through Coquihalla Pass after only 43 years of active life.

Geotechnical engineers surveying a route for the Coquihalla Highway in the early 1960s could hardly believe that the railwaymen had built a rail line through there in 1912. The scree makes what might be the least preferable base possible upon which to build anything, especially in an area subjected to massive doses of snow as this one was.[36] Scree usually assumes a much steeper slope than gravel or earth, as the jagged edges of the rock fragments snag on each other. This holding-together can be quite precarious at times, and scree will slide occasionally on its own, even without the addition of a heavy snow cover. If the snow stays it will become ice and the ice will hold things together until it thaws in the spring; then everything becomes mobile again. The presence of the rock fragments testifies to the instability of the rock faces above, which continually shed more rock when they are not shedding snow.

The transition point from semi-solid rock to scree was on a level remarkably close to that on which the track would eventually be built. All the workers had to do was cut out half the railbed width in the rock and support the other half on the scree. It was a cost-saving expedient if not a permanent one.

The only fully stable sections of the line were the trestles, which were built on bedrock, and the numerous small tunnels, as shown on the map "One Railway in a Canyon." In desperation, to combat constant instability problems in the fills, grasshopper trestles were built. Some of these were founded not in bedrock but on the scree farther down and they became the famous "moving trestles" of the line, which gradually and continuously slid down the slope and required constant adjustment. The railway grade was never really

This shows what was left of the town of Fernie after the holocaust of 1908. The morning after, J.J. Hill phoned Fernie's mayor with an offer of $5000 from his personal bank account to assist the burned-out citizens. The upper photo shows the roof of the Opera House blown off and carried a block. The lower photo is the Catholic Church, which was also destroyed by the fire behind.

finished throughout the canyon. There was constant ballasting to replace settling, and a regular need to rebuild slides and dig out rockfalls. In ten miles there were six snowsheds, six tunnels, and five trestles.[37]

✷ ✷ ✷

Jim Hill died on May 29, 1916, just two months before the Coquihalla Pass section opened. His son Louis made one trip over the Coquihalla Pass from Seattle to Spokane, travelling between Sumas and Hope on track that the VV&E shared with the Canadian Northern Pacific Railway under an agreement Hill negotiated with William Mackenzie and Donald Mann. This agreement granted that pair a valuable entry into Vancouver.

The GN never operated from Princeton to Vancouver as Jim Hill had so fervently hoped it would.[38] A few decades later Jim Hill's railway had to sit down with the CPR and the CNR to work out an agreement, a very onerous one for the GN, by which that railway finally withdrew from its responsibilities vis-à-vis the KVR. Louis Hill's single trip over the shared track was a very expensive one. Throughout the 1930s it was the GN's payment of rent for the Coquihalla line, which it never again used, that kept the KVR going.[39]

After the KVR/GN agreement of 1912, Allison Pass was cleared for road use. When the war ended in 1918 a line was run from Hope, over the Sumallo summit to the Skagit River by way of Skagit Bluffs, and on through Allison Pass to Princeton, where the highway runs now. That survey confirmed that Skagit Bluffs were by no means insurmountable, proving construction difficulties on the Allison Pass route were not the reason Gibson Pass had been chosen as the road route in 1910. Nothing else was done and then the Great Depression overtook the Department of Public Works and closed down all new construction. The key period to link Hope to Princeton was the early 1920s, but at that time they were only surveying, not building, a crucial transposition.

It is impossible to say with any accuracy what might have happened if the railway had not intervened, especially in the face of

These views are of the same snowshed, which is the only one remaining on the line of the Kettle Valley Railway between Brookmere and Hope. It is located within the upper Coquihalla Canyon alongside what is now an oil pipeline access road built on the old railway grade. The view in winter was taken from a helicopter used by the Department of Highways to survey the Coquihalla route in 1972, primarily to site weather recording stations. These were set up in 1973, and they have been recording snowfall and other information ever since. The view in summer shows that rocks often slid down as well as snow. The shed was originally of timber construction; it was converted to steel and concrete not long before the line ceased operating in 1955. Both photographs present graphic evidence that the upper canyon of the Coquihalla was a good place to stay away from, especially in winter.

a war and economic depression. The abandonment of work done on the west end of the Gibson Pass line must have lessened any enthusiasm to start another route after World War I. Had construction started on the Allison Pass route originally, the missing link might have been completed before the Depression really took hold, and B.C. would have had a road from Hope to Princeton twenty years earlier. This would certainly have helped the newly born British Columbia trucking industry, which at that time was struggling on very circuitous routes throughout the Interior. The lack of a direct road link from the coast to the southern Okanagan and Boundary regions, combined with the flooding and slide problems that plagued the Okanagan Lakeshore Road, provided a

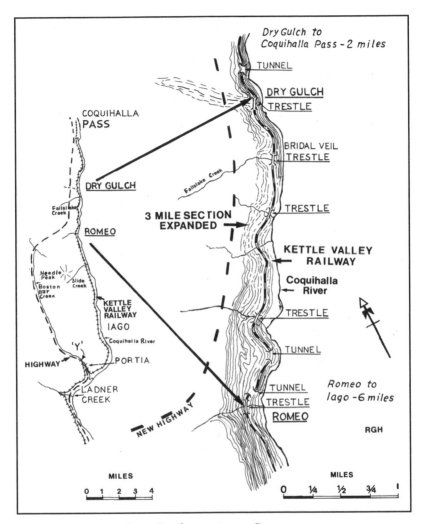

Dry Gulch to
Coquihalla Pass - 2 miles

TUNNEL

DRY GULCH
TRESTLE

COQUIHALLA
PASS

BRIDAL VEIL
TRESTLE

Fallslake Creek

TRESTLE

DRY GULCH

3 MILE SECTION
EXPANDED

ROMEO

Fallslake
Creek

KETTLE VALLEY
RAILWAY

Coquihalla
River

Needle
Peak   Slide
Boston   Creek
Bar
Creek

KETTLE
VALLEY
RAILWAY

TRESTLE

IAGO

'Y'   Coquihalla River

TUNNEL

HIGHWAY   PORTIA

LADNER
CREEK

TUNNEL   Romeo to
TRESTLE   Iago - 6 miles

NEW HIGHWAY

ROMEO

RGH

MILES

0 1 2 3 4

MILES

0   ¼   ½   ¾   1

One Railway in a Canyon

This plan shows the worst three miles of the Kettle Valley Railway through the fourteen-mile length of the upper Coquihalla Canyon, which stretches from one mile below twin Coquihalla Lakes to Ladner Creek. Between Romeo and Iago lay the steepest slopes above the track, at times reaching 45 degrees to the horizontal and rising up from 600 to 1000 metres in height. These slopes generated frequent snow and talus slides. The railway put in six snowsheds in this section, with an average length of 200 metres. There were also six tunnels of similar length, and five trestles in these ten miles.

gift from heaven for the CPR steamboats on Okanagan Lake and for the Kettle Valley Railway.

If a railway had continued to operate from Princeton to Hope up to present times, there are several conclusions that can be drawn. Firstly, if the Kettle Valley line were still in place it would have been near to impossible to build the Coquihalla Highway as it is today—although anything is possible if you are willing to spend enough. On the other hand, a GN line running through the Railroad

---

A note on snow conditions and a problem in the upper Coquihalla Canyon

The advantage of locating railways or highways on slopes with a southern exposure has been mentioned. In western Canada, particularly in regions of 50 or more degrees north latitude, the winter sun follows a very low arc in the southern and western sky. Among high mountain slopes, only those facing south see the sun for lengthy periods in the short days. Those facing north see little or none of it. Heavy snow cover in constant shadow not only does not melt, but the crusting in times of hard freezing also produces ice lenses with softer snow in between. There is far less likelihood of lenses forming on a south-facing slope. In periods of above-freezing weather, meltwater percolates down and lubricates these ice lenses, which may cause slab movement. At times this movement can turn into wild, loose-snow avalanches. It is hard to forecast when this progression will happen, but locating on a slope with a southern exposure means it is less likely to occur.

"One Railway in a Canyon" shows that, if nothing else, the KVR line through the upper Coquihalla Canyon had a suitable exposure. When J.J. Hill's men first surveyed that area they went on the other side of the canyon, a line that would have seldom seen the sun in winter. It is speculation, but possibly the trouble experienced by the CPR in Rogers Pass, particularly the disaster in 1910, drew attention to the need to favour the sunny side of mountain passes. This in turn may have led Hill to attempt to move his line to the other side. However the KVR had already filed on that side in Ottawa, and a Canadian court upheld its precedence. This was a major reason for Hill's capitulation.

Pass tunnel and along the left bank of the Coquihalla River on its lower reach to Hope would not have interfered with the highway in any way, and in this case the railway would not have been there at all from Brookmere to Portia.

Hal Riegger opines that the alignment and nature of the mountain ranges immediately north of the U.S. border rule out an east-west rail line. Certainly many of the photographs in his book support that conclusion. They show more than a dozen huge trestle structures and lofty spans soaring over a hundred feet above the floors of the ravines along the Kettle Valley Railway route from the Kettle River to the Okanagan and on to Princeton.

The apex of the KVR problem was the Coquihalla Pass and the upper canyon. Railway historians describe vividly the extreme snowfalls that brought havoc to both the pass and upper canyon following the opening in 1916 and throughout the 1930s. Washouts and slippage occurred then and later. The line survived storms of great intensity, both economic and celestial, and a second world war, but it was finally proven to be unmaintainable at a reasonable cost. The last train rolled to a stop on November 23, 1959, shutting down the line after 43 years of operation.

It is difficult to find fault with a man like Andrew McCulloch. He showed his surveying ability and railway know-how in building the Quintette Tunnels, which fortunately are being preserved. However it cannot be ignored that only 12 percent of the 163 miles of the KVR between Penticton and Hope were built in the right place—those from Dewdney Creek westwards. The line should have taken the Similkameen and Tulameen valleys, then tunnelled under Railroad Pass to Dewdney Creek. McCulloch should have avoided the upper canyon of the Coquihalla, and had he held out strongly for the Railroad Pass route, especially in view of Jim Hill having called tenders for the tunnel there, compromise with the GNR could have come years earlier. A joint line might have been built on that basis.

The final verdict on the railway built along B.C.'s southern border and challenging the mountain ranges came from the CPR

This looks like one tunnel, but it is actually a view of two out of four—and to complicate things even further they are called the Quintette Tunnels! Either the namer was confused or he liked the word quintette better than quartette (or he wanted to be one up on the opposition). The tunnels are on the Kettle Valley Railway in the lower canyon of the Coquihalla River a few miles outside of Hope. Two of the three gaps between the tunnels contain bridge crossings of the river, surrounded by brutally steep rock walls confining the river to less than a quarter of its normal width. The surveying and rock drilling of Andrew McCulloch's masterpiece had to be done by men suspended in bosun's chairs by ropes from above. These tunnels—556, 100, 405, and 246 feet long, progressing from the east—can presently be viewed by the public from a trail within a land reserve established by the B.C. Ministry of Lands and Parks. The bridges are 75 and 175 feet long, and one is shown in the foreground. All four tunnels and two bridges are in a straight line.

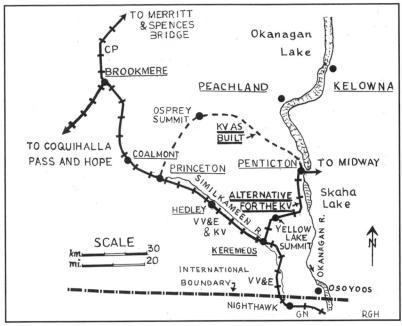

A Much Easier Way from Penticton to Princeton

Two professionals could have aided Andrew McCulloch before he committed himself to his route westwards from Penticton. There were good arguments against the Osprey Summit route he followed with his Kettle Valley Railway and in favour of one by Yellow Lake Summit, 1100 feet lower in altitude.

A meteorologist would have compared the climate of the upper plateau around Osprey Lake with that of Hedley. Six months with freezing temperatures instead of four—a difference of 15 degrees Fahrenheit in maximum low temperature in a normal winter—and a mean annual temperature of 34 degrees on the plateau compared to 47 degrees at Hedley. As well, the high plateau is subject to sustained winds (and a vicious wind chill) in winter, leading to constant drifting of snow and treacherous icing conditions.

As early as 1902 an economic geographer would note the agricultural value of the lower Similkameen Valley and the existing road from Fairview to Hedley, home to a sawmill and the highly successful Nickel Plate Mine, soon to be a good customer for the GNR.

Unfortunately, the KVR builders first decided to bypass Princeton and go directly west from Osprey by Aspen Grove to the Coldwater valley. This was when the above debate should have taken place. The second, and last-minute, decision to go south to Princeton simply underlined the problem.

itself. Writing to Chief Engineer McCulloch on March 2, 1937, a senior official of the company expressed himself with an unusual directness: "Of all the blunders in railway building history the CPR's southern British Columbia rail line is the greatest." (He obviously put it all together, Crowsnest Pass to Hope.) He must have been an accountant, as only an accountant would have written to the revered Andrew McCulloch in that manner, and he probably wrote the letter after he had reached the bottom line of the KVR ledger after twenty years of operation. While that railway often posted an operating profit, it never approached a return sufficient to retire the massive capital construction investment.[40]

But they both did wonders for British Columbia: the railway that wed itself to the province so hastily and the highway that followed it so tardily.

A PLACE CALLED PORTIA

At the junction of Boston Bar Creek and the Coquihalla River, Portia, an operational centre of the KVR, was named by Chief Engineer Andrew McCulloch's daughter after a William Shakespeare character. Portia sits on flat land just upstream of a 150-foot-deep canyon. Here the KVR built a 'Y' to turn around snowplough trains when they had to make continuous trips back and forth between Portia and Coquihalla Pass. It is a remarkable crossroad in B.C.'s transportation history.

Back in 1846, Alexander Caulfield Anderson, the jack-of-all-trades of the Hudson's Bay Company, came through here in his rather desperate search for a usable route for the fur brigades between Fort Kamloops and Fort Langley after Fort Vancouver in Oregon was barred to them by treaty. Anderson went up Boston Bar Creek valley to a point close to Box Canyon and then crossed over the high ridge of mountains parallel to the right bank of the creek. There he found and followed a river, later to be named after him, which flows westwards down to the Fraser River.

In 1859, Lieutenant Arthur Lempriere of Her Majesty's Corps of Royal Engineers retraced Anderson's footsteps through Portia. He led a party of sappers and settlers from Fort Hope. The civilians wanted to help him build a wagon road to Boston Bar and on to Fort Kamloops, as they greatly desired to make their town the river port for the Interior. Lempriere looked at "signs of fearsome snowfalls" on the mountains either side of Boston Bar Creek and ruled out any carriageways by this route. Instead the engineers built their famous wagon road through the Fraser Canyon, starting from Yale.[41]

Then in 1872 work commenced building a cattle trail from Hope up the Coquihalla River through Portia, through Coquihalla Pass, and on down to Nicola Forks, the site of the present-day town of Merritt. This six-foot-wide trail was completed in four years, and the work went ahead despite warnings from bureaucrats in the Department of Lands and Works that the trailbuilders had to cross "a very bad rocky slide composed of immense fragments of granite." The commissioner at that time was pioneer cattle rancher Forbes George Vernon. Naturally he overruled these niggling objections and completed the trail. It was destroyed by the building of the Kettle Valley Railway in 1913.[42]

After the railway shut down in 1959, two pipeline companies came through Portia, building a gas pipeline and two oil pipelines from Hope to Merritt. The single gas pipeline went by Boston Bar Creek valley, and the double oil pipelines by the Coquihalla valley. Portia was once again a crossroad. Finally in 1986 the four-lane mountain freeway called the Coquihalla Highway was completed through Portia, up the Boston Bar Creek valley, through the Great Bear Snowshed at its headwaters, and on through Coquihalla Pass to Merritt.

Chapter 6

The Okanagan Valley

CPR sternwheelers distribute would-be fruit growers along a road-poor shoreline

Immigration to the Okanagan Valley at a rate larger than a trickle took place between the years 1898 and 1914, and although the population has grown steadily since then, this was certainly the burst of energy that got the valley going. What occurred was one of the greatest long-distance land-selling operations ever staged, and one of the most successful. It is also one of the most interesting episodes of B.C.'s early history.

It took a lot of nerve to recruit immigrants on a large scale, primarily in Britain; transport them to the Okanagan Valley; sell them land there; and hopefully, but not necessarily, watch them survive and prosper thereafter from their own resources and by their own efforts. A lot of things had to come together to make this campaign successful; fortunately they did. It took:

1. A steamship service across the Atlantic Ocean, and a railway across the continent.
2. An agency within Great Britain to advertise and promote the emigration.
3. Connecting transportation from the CPR mainline to the valley and lake.
4. Sympathetic provincial and national governments.
5. Available land and facilities, and the potential for the immigrants to earn a living.
6. An energetic and efficient sales force.

To go through the above list, the first requirement was of course provided by the Canadian Pacific's railway and steamship empire, about which little needs to be said. The second, a contact in London, was met by B.C.'s agent-general. By good fortune the man in that office when they needed him was a recently retired premier of the province who was still in good standing with those in power.[1] John Herbert Turner, who had been B.C.'s premier from March 1895 to August 1898, was, according to a biographer, "a distinguished gentleman with a swift and snappy walk, head erect, and body well poised"; when it came to promoting British Columbia it seemed that he had a smart mind to go along with these outward attributes. He started the promotion of agriculture in B.C. during his term as premier, when it became obvious how successfully the national railway was attracting settlers to the prairies with grants of land. He continued to promote agriculture and settlement diligently when he became agent-general.[2]

The Canadian Pacific Railway had endorsed Turner's forward-looking policies, and nobody appreciated them better than its president, Thomas Shaughnessy. Early in the new century he introduced the amazingly low fare of $40 to Canada, a material support if there ever was one to emigration to British Columbia. After that the scheme to fill the Okanagan Valley with people was under way in high gear.[3]

The beautiful scenery of western Canada was proving to be a powerful magnet for bringing people with financial resources to the area, if only as tourists. These were also the type of person B.C. preferred as immigrants or investors over those who only brought their hands to sustain them. Where was there more beautiful scenery in British Columbia than in the Okanagan? One man who saw that valley and thereafter praised it consistently was the Canadian Governor-General of the period, Lord Aberdeen, and he eventually did a lot more about it than that.[4] As it turned out, these three men—Turner, Shaughnessy, and Aberdeen—were to be the underpinning of the effort to achieve a much denser population in the Okanagan Valley.

The next necessity was the provision of connecting transportation from the CPR line to the lake area, and here some very opportune local enterprise came into play. The same year that the CPR mainline was completed, a syndicate of Okanagan businessmen applied to the provincial government for a charter to build a connecting rail line south from the mainline to the Okanagan Valley, and with good sense they terminated it at the head of the lake.[5] The man who conceived this railway was Moses Lumby, who eventually became the government agent at Vernon (its neighbouring town was named after him). A major investor with Lumby was Forbes George Vernon, about whom more is told later.[6]

Thus the Shuswap and Okanagan Railway Company came into being, and by 1892 the line was fully operational from Sicamous Junction to Okanagan Landing. It was not much of a railway to start with, having only one passenger car that was described as being rather like an oversized bus.[7] Trains ran very slowly as it was necessary to shoo cows off the line from time to time. As well, local farmers who filled boxcars on sidings with produce found them forgotten rather regularly, so they fell into the practice of moving the cars onto the mainline to get better attention. Not surprisingly this caused considerable backing and filling.

Paddy Acland, in conversation for the B.C. Archives' Aural History Program, described the S&O as he first encountered it on his way to the Okanagan early in this century. He said, "Well, you could walk down [from Sicamous] almost as quick as you came by that train: it stopped everywhere." Alex Lord confirms this in his book.[8]

As might be anticipated, this rail line was very soon purchased by the CPR and after that it never looked back—nor forward for cars on the track.

As soon as the local railway came into the fold, the CPR laid the keel for the next link in the transportation chain: a craft to use the lake, built on ways laid down at Okanagan Landing. One year after the steam whistle of the S&O first echoed across these waters, the lake's depths were parted by the graceful bow of the *Aberdeen*, the Okanagan's first sternwheeler. By this symbiosis of railway and lakecraft the CPR brought the people to the lake and showed it to them by the best means possible.[9]

Returning to the list and looking at item four, this proved to be the easiest of all. With Turner's contacts provincially, Shaughnessy's access to the dominion government, and Governor-General Lord Aberdeen's interest, the sympathetic support of the provincial and national governments was assured.

Finally, to deal with the last two items and to explain how so much suitable land became available for sale in the Okanagan Valley at that particular time, it is necessary to delve a little more into the history of the valley. Here again, three men stand out.

They are, in the order of their arrival, Father Charles Pandosy, an oblate missionary of the Catholic Church; Forbes George Vernon, an amiable old-country adventurer bent on ranching, accompanied in this by his elder brother Charles; and Thomas Ellis, an Irish farmer of keen intellect. They arrived between the years 1859 and 1865, and to save a lot of unnecessary verbiage their departures were as follows. Father Pandosy died in 1891, Tom Ellis retired in 1906, and Forbes Vernon, who became a noted provincial politician and holder of high office, preceded Turner as agent-general for British Columbia in London in 1894 and left that office to stay in England in 1898.

Although they were in the valley nearly simultaneously, these three men represented two very different ways of life, one which came in and one which departed. Pandosy represented the missionaries who carried on from the fur traders. Vernon and Ellis represented the cattlemen who bridged the gap from preaching the word of God in the wilderness to settled agriculture.

Father Pandosy projected an image of the white man that calmed the Native peoples, who had taken a long time to forget the disastrous intrusion of the American miners in 1858, a serious disturbance to them after their good relationship with the Hudson's Bay men.[10] He showed them that the white man was not all bad, that he had humility and patience to go along with the arrogance

The Aberdeen *at full speed ahead is flying the CPR's British Columbia Lake and River Service flag. It is a chequerboard of red and white squares, and woe betide any captain who flew it without the single red square up. Cynics compared it to the race-winning chequerboard and said it was chosen because the CPR won out by eliminating all the competition.*

Father Pandosy (left) and his church at Okanagan Mission (above, c. 1896). Father Charles Pandosy was a Catholic missionary of the oblate order. He arrived in the Okanagan in 1859 and established the first permanent white settlement at Okanagan Mission. He tended to the Native people of the area and encouraged white settlement. Pandosy travelled constantly, fulfilling his missionary duties admirably until his death in 1891. He is remembered by a street named after him in Kelowna and by a ferry misspelled the Pandozi.

and self-importance they saw at times with the HBC men, and that he had kindness to offset the belligerence of the gold-rush hordes. Father Pandosy also taught their children and travelled the area doing his good works, and his importance was immense. Among other things, he was the first apple grower and earned the nickname "Apple Pandosy" for it. The Indian Mission, which stood where the city of Kelowna now stands, with Eli Lequime's store and Mrs. Lequime's medicine chest alongside it, and Theodore Kruger's store and tavern at Osoyoos, were about the only centres of care and sustenance in an unpopulated paradise of far-flung ranches.[11]

The Honourable Forbes George Vernon was Chief Commissioner of Lands and Works for British Columbia from 1876 to 1878, and again from 1887 to 1895.

Tom Ellis, known as the king of the Okanagan cattlemen, was outstanding because of his ability to acquire property and put abandoned land to good use. In this he was not only astute but also lucky. He came into possession of a huge acreage when his friend John Carmichael Haynes died, purchasing it along with 1200 head of cattle to add to the 4000 he already had. (Haynes, another Irishman, was a civil servant who acquired land as a sideline.) Ellis was also the man on the spot when a large Native reserve was dissolved near Penticton, and his holdings grew greatly from that. It was said that the king's royal realm spread from fifteen miles north of Penticton all the way to Osoyoos.[12]

When he retired, Ellis owned 40,000 acres and had grazing rights covering another 30,000 acres. That he acquired all of this, and at the easiest of terms for the public land, is more of a discredit to the political system in Victoria, which let it happen, than anything else, and no one can blame him for taking advantage of it. There were other ranchers in the Okanagan, most of them not quite so blessed with land as was Ellis, but nonetheless successful. Cornelius O'Keefe was one, and Price Ellison another, and both became legends in the history of the area. On the other hand there was the unsuccessful John Allison, who stayed only a few years but whose name became more historically noted than any of them.[13]

Captain Thomas Dolman Shorts was a likeable man who provided water transportation with a notable lack of ceremony—or regularity. He was first on the scene in 1883, rowing when his sails did not work, then bowing to steam. He went off to the Klondike in 1898 and forgot to come back. He died at Hope in 1921 aged 84.

Ellis kept his contribution to transportation in the Okanagan area quiet, for good reason. For a time he financially supported the highly individualistic Thomas Dolman Shorts, who provided the first steamboat service on the lake between the years 1886 and 1897, an infrequent and uncertain operation. Captain Shorts, who started off rowing the length of the lake in a 22-foot boat before he turned to steam, thoroughly disliked routine, a bad trait in a ferryman, and his arrival at the various landings was charitably described as "semi-occasional."[14] His was not an operation that you would admit to backing.

Forbes Vernon was one of the most successful politicians of his time. There is little doubt that a natural joviality can do great things, and this along with a keen mind and an ability to get along with almost anyone were his keys to success. In no other way could he have survived in the crucial position of Chief Commissioner of Lands and Works in the provincial government under three separate premiers in the fourth quarter of the last century. He was chief commissioner under Premier Arthur Charles Elliot in 1876, Premier Alexander E. B. Davie in 1887, and Premier John Robson in 1889.

In 1873 he and his brother purchased the holding of Colonel Charles Frederick Houghton, the property known as the Coldstream Ranch. When Vernon controlled both the administration of provincial lands and the creation of access to them, he looked after his Okanagan homelands and those of his neighbours very well indeed. Prominent in his priorities was a good road from Kamloops to Vernon (a centre later named after him) and on to Kelowna, and he pursued this diligently, to the frustration of the settlers on the west side of the lake, who got nothing.[15]

He ingratiated himself with others of his calling by pushing through a cattle trail from Hope to Merritt via the Coquihalla Pass, as mentioned in the previous chapter. He was a cattleman's cattleman and was also a power in the land. In his lifetime he accumulated 13,000 acres at Vernon, the sale of which was the trigger to "Operation Population" in the Okanagan Valley because he sold his ranch to Lord Aberdeen, and his lordship had every intention of becoming a land developer as well as a rancher. More importantly, Aberdeen had capital and the aristocratic influence in Britain to encourage his countrymen to follow his example.[16]

So this was how suitable land became available. The pioneer ranchers had lots of acreage and were willing to sell because they were at the time of life when they wished to turn away from the hard work of raising cattle. They were helped on their way by the aristocratic Scotsman who had also acquired the Guisachan Ranch near Kelowna. That 500-acre estate was his first purchase.

The real estate agent who arranged these substantial deals for his lordship was one of the first to demonstrate the remarkable salesmanship widely seen in western Canada in these years. This man, G.G. MacKay, organized the Okanagan Land and Development Company. MacKay's prime source of clients was the Vancouver area. He was soon joined in the business of turning cattleland into dollars by a man called John Robinson, who picked up the Lambley ranch and organized the Summerland Development Company, promptly selling twenty acres at Peachland to Thomas Shaughnessy and making him president of the company. Another investor was Charles R. Hosmer, the manager of CPR Telegraphs and a director of the railway company. Robinson spent half the year in Manitoba, where he found his land buyers.

Another in the field was W.T. Shatford, whose South Okanagan Land Company obtained an option on the Ellis estate in 1905. The entire holding was subdivided and sold. There was the Kelowna Land and Orchard Company, and the Belgo-Canadian Fruit Land Co. These entrepreneurs, and others following them, more than filled the requirement of an energetic and efficient sales force.[17]

Finally there was the question "How would they all make a living?" The answer was simple: they would exploit the marvellous capacity of the land to support orchards, the fruit from which would, according to the salesmen, keep each and every one of them on easy street for life. One of the pioneers' daughters, Effie McGuire, when interviewed for the Aural History Program, said that this message was delivered to her father personally by no less a person than the agent-general ex-premier in London. Her father, John Kidston, came out to B.C. in 1904 with his wife and five children. Turner told Kidston that all he had to do was come out, buy his land, and have enough money left over for eight to ten years' sustenance until the fruit trees were bearing. Then he would be in clover for life. McGuire said, "It didn't work out that way!" But Kidston had no regrets.[18]

By 1907 the gun had fired and the rush was on. One million fruit trees were planted in the Okanagan Valley south of Vernon that year—in 1902 a killing frost had demolished all the fruit trees north of that centre. (It must have been an exceptional winter, as temperatures down to −30 degrees Fahrenheit are not unknown in Vernon, and there are many orchards there today, but of course they have smudge pots now.) It was said that the price of land around the lakeshore rose almost overnight from one dollar an acre to a thousand dollars an acre, which shows the power of multiple land development companies operating at full throttle.

Over 30 landings were created around the shores of Okanagan Lake to serve the *Aberdeen* and its colleague, the longer and larger

This view of Okanagan Landing in 1904, with the Aberdeen "docked," shows that even at CP's base of lake operations, their shoreside establishment was minimal.

This picture of Kelowna in 1905 demonstrates that high wooden sidewalks may be hard to step up to out of the mud, but they were handy for stepping out of a buggy.

This is the Okanagan *in April 1907, about to be baptized. Even from the outside it looks ornate, and the magnificence inside was greeted with rapture. The higher-class cabins were reportedly finished in gold and enamel, but surely it was not pure gold. The dining-room sideboard was of Australian cedar. The boat was a success.*

and more luxurious *Okanagan*, which was launched that year. A landing was created at any point where the settlement stretched out for a mile or two, and very soon the government would follow that with a dock. Ewings Landing, Fintry, Nahun, Caesars Landing, Wilsons Landing, and such better-known places as Summerland, Peachland, Westbank, and Naramata appeared on the map.[19] Everyone was happy.

Everyone, that is, except the road authority—but it did not have time to think about roads before the bubble burst in 1913. The man who blew away the Okanagan land boom was his Germanic majesty Kaiser Wilhelm II, and he did not have to fire a shot. His armour rattling frightened the skittish English overseas investors to the critical point before any guns fired in Belgium or France, and their money evaporated. It was these guns and the men killed by them a year or two later that took the blush off the rose of Interior settlement in British Columbia, and it would be a few years before it came back. In some areas, such as Walhachin, farther north on the Thompson River, it never did.[20]

When these events on the other side of the world slowed settlement, the men and women living in these remote communities took a look around and realized they needed roads, properly maintained roads, not only within their communities but also to connect them to the provincial network. Roadbuilding came under the responsibility of the district road superintendent, who was much more of a local politician than an administrator in these days. Some funds were sent into the area by the provincial government, mostly for administration or special work asked for by the elected representative, but primarily the roads came from the pre-emption of land—the settlers received land in exchange for a promise to work on the roads that would serve it. The district road superintendent appointed or elected a farmer in each location as the local road foreman, and put him to work directing his fellow settlers to build the roads, either as a qualification for pre-emption or in payment of their taxes. This was a much more suitable system for sodbusters on the prairies than for English immigrants who were struggling along as amateur fruit growers, a fact reflected in the quality of the roads produced.

Around Okanagan Lake, the problem of joining up the lake landings was caused by the nature of the terrain between them. It was full of terraces and benches formed in the glacial age, with some steep-sided hills and valleys mixed in. This was particularly evident along the west side of the lake from Westbank to Penticton, and northwards from Westbank to Ewings Landing. The landings were all in low-lying areas, so building roads was literally an uphill task. Another problem was flooding, as the roads were of necessity very close to lake level near the landings. A survey between Penticton and Peachland made in February 1918 by W.G. Gwyer, the Public Works district engineer, showed that 11 of the 26 miles were within six feet or less of the normal high-water level, and February was the month of lowest water.[21]

All of these headaches were increased substantially in the 1920s and for some years afterwards by the actions of local officials of the dominion government, those in charge of the Experimental Farm that Ottawa had established a few miles north of Penticton. One thing these agricultural researchers were promoting was irrigation, and they watered so intensely to show good results that they caused landslides on the edge of the benches above Lakeshore Road, as Highway 95 was called in these days. This situation persisted right through to 1943, by which time there had been a total of 25 slides, some closing the road for three weeks at a time.[22]

So the dominion government and the fruit industry added to the original problems caused by the CPR, its sternwheelers, and land promotion. Amidst all of this the influx of Britishers continued, although slowed down somewhat by the war. They encountered the ultimate in lake service luxury with the *Sicamous*, launched in June 1914, wherein they sat down to five-course dinners with spotless white table linen, glittering silverware, and the finest wines. With many windows and upholstered chairs from which to view the lovely surroundings, along with carpeted floors and other extravagances, the immigrants from England got a taste of home,

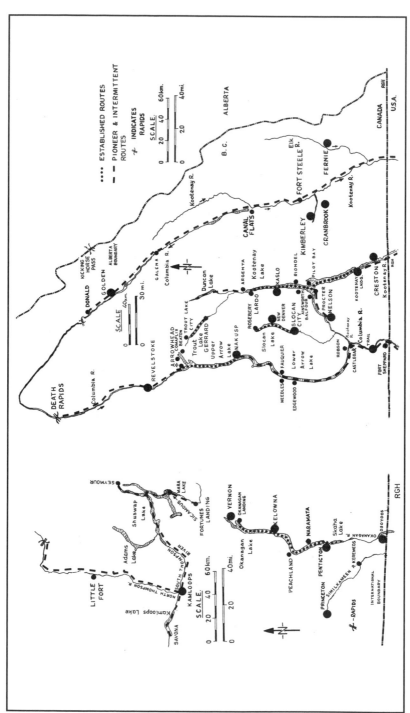

Routes of the Sternwheelers

ROUTES OF THE STERNWHEELERS

The CPR's British Columbia Lake and River Service became a monopoly on British Columbia's southern Interior lakes and rivers (except in the Thompson River watershed) early in the 1900s. A sense of winning pervaded the service—after all, had it not forced the withdrawal of Jim Hill's Great Northern Railway from the south? Even the house flag, a chequerboard like the one waved at a winning motor racer, expressed this dominance. The only difference was that the CPR Lake and River Service's flag was three red and three white squares. The Service considered it essential that the flag be flown right side up, with a red square in the centre top—and woe betide any captain who flew it incorrectly.

From Savona to Fortune's Landing via Kamloops Lake, Thompson and South Thompson Rivers, Shuswap Lake, and Shuswap River is 140 miles, with an extra 17 miles to Seymour. Service began in 1858 and the Thompson saw its last sternwheeler in 1948.

Okanagan Lake, 69 miles in length, saw its first sternwheeler in 1893 and its last in 1931, with tug and barge service there until 1972.

Navigation on 22-mile Slocan Lake started in 1897 and sternwheelers ceased in 1928. Passenger tugs ran until 1958. Trout Lake sternwheelers operated on a 13-mile route from 1900 to 1904. Passenger tugs served until 1921.

The Columbia River was navigable from Kettle Falls, 35 miles south of the border, to Death Rapids, 65 miles upstream of Revelstoke. Steamboating over that entire 260-mile stretch started in 1856, though in 1893 it became limited to the section from Trail to Arrowhead. The final vessel on the route was the Minto, beached in 1954. The upper Columbia River is navigable from the rapids above Donald to Columbia Lake at Canal Flats, a distance of 130 miles. Sternwheeler navigation started on the upper Columbia River in 1886 and lasted until 1920.

The upper Kootenay River is navigable for 150 miles from Canal Flats to Jennings, Montana. Sternwheelers on the upper Kootenay started in May 1893, but decreased substantially when the B.C. Southern Railway came into service from Lethbridge to Nelson late in 1898. Navigation on the upper Kootenay River ended in 1902.

Kootenay Lake is navigable for its entire 65-mile length and for the 20-mile west arm to Nelson. The lower Kootenay River is navigable from south of the lake, 27 miles to the border and upstream as far as Bonners Ferry, Idaho, another 25 miles. Sternwheeler service on Kootenay Lake started in 1891, and steamboat service in 1884. This service extended at times to Duncan Lake, which added another 30 miles. The last sternwheeler moved on Kootenay Lake on April 27, 1957, with tug and barge service lasting until 1977.

and the contrast with other modes of transportation was enough to render the old-timers speechless.[23]

One of the most poignant photographs taken in that period was of the *Sicamous* at the pier at Kelowna in 1914. Framed by the decks and stanchions are 1000 young men, Kelowna's gift to the war in Europe. As they look down upon their township, which tragically few would see again, a huge crowd of several times their number looks back. Only 22 years before that, the entire population of the Okanagan Valley was estimated at not more than 500 white settlers, as well as 20,000 cattle.[24] In the 50 years from 1865 to 1915 the area's population shifted from fur traders to missionaries, then cattlemen, and finally an assortment of fruit-farmers, tradespeople, and retirees, with a fast-growing tourist trade.

The final word on the gentlemen immigrants of the Okanagan early in this century is from an official of Canada's Department of Immigration and Colonisation in the east, who dealt with the influx every day and finally put his feelings into verse.

> He is brand new out of England and he thinks
>   he knows it all
> There's a blooming bit of boggle in his eye.
> The colonial who crosses him is going to get a fall,
> There's a seven-pound revolver on his thigh.
> He's a son of Marquis Noddle, he's the nephew of an earl,
> In the social swim of England he has had them all awhirl.
> He's as confident as Caesar, and as pretty as a girl—
> Oh, he's out in deadly earnest, do or die.[25]

The *Sicamous* was launched just before the war, and when those of the volunteers who survived the trenches returned to the Okanagan, they had changed and so had the province. One of the most potent innovations was the automobile. Only available to the rich before the war, thanks to Henry Ford it became something quite different afterwards. Between 1912 and 1914 he created the first mass production line for his Model T cars, and by 1925 one was emerging every fifteen seconds. In 1907 there were 107 horseless

BUCKED, TRIMMED, AND SHIPPED OUT

In case the reader has gained the impression that conditions for immigrants to B.C. in the early years of this century were all sunny shores and palatial sternwheelers, that was far from the truth, and more so if the immigrant did not speak English.

This author's father was the first city engineer of Duncan on Vancouver Island, appointed in 1913, and he reported that one logging operation at Cowichan Lake on the Island would offer jobs to the lowly immigrants stepping off the train in Vancouver. They were often most willing to take this offer and were quickly signed up and transported by CPR ship to Victoria, by Esquimalt & Nanaimo railroad to Duncan, and by specially arranged horse-and-carriage service to the lake. A leading citizen of Duncan, who was also a city council member, provided that service.

The new workers were outfitted at the company store on credit and were also provided with room and board. After a month of backbreaking toil, most asked to be paid off and a reckoning took place. On one side of the sheet were their fares by steamer, train, and carriage, none of which were insignificant. Then there were the charges for board and outfitting, also substantial. On the other side were their wages. When the two sides were balanced, there was little cash left over.

When the immigrants straggled down to Duncan and sought work, they were immediately threatened with prosecution for vagrancy and run out of town. The man who proposed the Duncan vagrancy by-law was that same leading citizen who provided transport to the logging camp.

Most of the men would find work in the Nanaimo area coal mines, but their satisfaction was probably tempered when they found out that James Dunsmuir's coal pits had twice the rate of death and injury per day at work as any equivalent mine in Britain.

The logging managers at Cowichan Lake treated their immigrant labour very much as they handled their trees. After they were felled they were cut to size (bucked), then they were relieved of accoutrements (trimmed), and finally they were shipped out.

carriages registered in British Columbia, many of them steam-powered. By 1920 there were 28,000 motor vehicles registered. Five years later this number had doubled to 56,427 and by 1930 to 98,938, after which it slowed due to the Depression.[26] In 1918 automobiles were issued to the Public Works Department district engineers; prior to that they had travelled over any long distance by rail or steamer. (District engineers took over from road superintendents during the war.)

The old song about the returned soldiers, "How're you going to keep them down on the farm, after they've seen Paree ?" in the Okanagan might have been rewritten, "How're you going to keep them down by the lake, after they've seen a Model T ?" People wanted cars, and therefore they wanted roads, and thanks mainly to the sternwheelers there were quite often no roads available in southern B.C., or else very poor ones.

Forbes George Vernon pushed through an eighteen-foot-wide gravel road to Kelowna from Kamloops by 1891, but south of that and across the lake there was a ten-mile gap north of Trout Creek due to "the need for blasting." This was overcome by 1907, but the result was nothing better than a rough wagon road all the way from Westside to Penticton. In 1914 the DPW files show that the road from Penticton to Keremeos was capable of handling automobiles, but correspondence in 1919 and for many years afterwards shows that the road from Kelowna to Penticton continued to be in very poor shape and was not recommended for cars. It was the forgotten link, and no one seemed to know why.[27]

It was both regrettable and ironic that in 1902 there was no through road down the west side of Okanagan Lake. Only 60 years had passed since a historic fur brigade trail in the same area had reached the peak of its usefulness. It ran the length of the lake on its west side. As there was no need to serve communities on the lakeshore at that time, this thoroughfare was located quite far back from the water and higher up. "High above the shining waters" was how one brigade captain referred to this trail in his journal. It was the fur export route from New Caledonia to the Pacific for

The Sicamous *on Okanagan Lake (top).   The lower photo shows the crew, c. 1928.*

twenty years, and the fur traders heartily deplored abandoning it for a route past Nicola Lake and over the mountains to Hope. This happened after Britain and the Hudson's Bay Company lost Oregon to the United States in 1846.[28]

N.S. Davidson of the Idylwylde Ranch at Trepanier, B.C., in a letter dated January 16, 1919, advised Minister of Public Works Dr. James Horace King that he had counted 162 curves on 20 miles of road between Peachland and Penticton (an average of one every 652 feet), 21 of them certainly dangerous, and he recounted that several automobiles had been smashed up in collisions in one section. This was not unlikely as the road there was subsequently measured as no wider than nine feet.[29]

The same Department of Public Works file yields evidence that some petitioners who wanted this road to be improved sought the support of the superintendent of the CPR, Richard Marpole. Asking the CPR to help improve a road that would assist its competition was like asking the Devil to show you the way to Heaven! The file does not treat the reader to Mr. Marpole's reply, but nothing much happened to the road.

The 1920s were a happy time for one means of travel in the area, as the Canadian Pacific British Columbia Lake and River Service prospered with its boat service on Okanagan Lake, mainly because the poor road on the west side discouraged transporting fruit by trucks or people by bus, so another CPR monopoly flourished. The opening of the Kettle Valley Railway in 1916 was a setback, as there was now a shorter route for traffic from Penticton eastbound for the mainline. A further blow to the lake service came from the CNR line that was built from Kamloops to Kelowna in 1926, a rather belated attempt to diminish the CPR hegemony.[30]

This was the writing on the wall, and in 1931 the CPR abruptly terminated the sternwheeler service on Okanagan Lake. This did not last for long, however, as pressure from the Okanagan Valley boards of trade, primarily aimed at the dominion government, eventually won a reprieve and the service was restored. The cost to the taxpayer was not revealed, but surely there was one. The reprieve

The CPR may not have had much in the way of facilities at Okanagan Landing, but it had all sorts and sizes of vessels as shown here. These range from the screw-driven tug York *(88 feet, 134 gross tons), which had passenger cabins, through the sternwheelers* Kaleden *(94 feet, 180 tons) and* Aberdeen *(146 feet, 544 tons), to the magnificent* Sicamous *(200.5 feet, 1787 tons). The* Sicamous *stands tall among its companions.*

was shortlived. By January 1935 the depression won out and the *Sicamous* was tied up for the last time.[31]

Later in that same year, road surveyors produced plans for a revision of the road that ran north of Penticton along the toe of the steep clay slopes or "hoodoos" as they were called. This line cut across the bays by the Experimental Farm, and it was possible to build the road on fills because the lake was so shallow there due to the mud flowing in for so many years. Lack of funding intervened again, however, and nothing happened until 1939 when the road went ahead as part of a 50/50 dominion-provincial highway building program for tourist promotion. The Okanagan Highway, as it was then known, never looked back thereafter, and by the end of 1940 it was paved throughout. An era was over.[32]

The last words come from two pioneers interviewed for the Aural History Program. J.B. Weeks had a long career as a mate and a captain for the CPR lake boats and he said:

> The combined CPR train and boat service played a large part in the opening up of the Okanagan Valley. It brought

in new settlers; it connected remote settlements; it carried freight, mail and supplies; it took fruit to market; and it served, to some extent, as a locus for social activity.

The inimitable Paddy Acland adds, "We had no roads. Travel was only possible by horseback on primitive roads or trails...or by boats."[33]

Captain J.B. Weeks was the best known of the lake skippers on Okanagan Lake. He retired in 1942 after 45 years of service on inland waterways. He logged over two million miles on Okanagan Lake.

Chapter 7

Arrow, Kootenay, and Slocan Lakes

Mining in the mountains and communities by the lakeside bring problems for the road builders

Early in the century there was a remarkable mixture of people living along the lakeshores and riverbanks of the southeastern corner of British Columbia. The sudden and exciting emergence of precious metals other than the elusive and often fickle placer gold brought permanence, mines and smelters and railways, and the work force to create and sustain the industry. Nearby, the sunny shores of Okanagan Lake enticed a rapidly enlarging community of fruit growers, and the overflow moved east. But the people who came to settle the shores of Kootenay Lake, Arrow Lake, the Slocan, and other areas of B.C. included more than just miners or those who wanted to grow peaches and live happily ever after. There was a most unusual group, one that British Columbians should treasure in memory and not let slip into the past: the remittance men.[1]

There were probably also remittance women, though they were never mentioned. The remittance men were just what their name implied: men in receipt of a remittance, money sent to them from their place of origin, usually from their family, to sustain them and often simply to keep them away from the family homestead, which included many of the most stately in Britain.

The remittance men were an offshoot of the strictures of Victorian and Edwardian society, more particularly of the English law of primogeniture, a grossly unfair statute that awarded the inheritance of the wealth and property of English families to the eldest son, and to him alone. Whatever a law may say, it cannot insure that the first born shall be the best. Often he was not, but the younger sons, or the daughters, had no recourse. If they kicked up too much fuss—and the situation encouraged that—what better to do than to send them far, far away? And British Columbia beckoned, the farthest of all. John Turner did the beckoning, and the CPR threw in a cheap fare, and off they went. Some of course were less than perfect in their outlook or habits, but a very large percentage of them were very fine citizens. This was proven in 1914 when so many of them volunteered to serve, and in many cases to die, for the country that had rejected them. Bob Edwards, the irrepressible editor of the *Calgary Eyeopener*, had the last word that year when he said, "They may have been green, but they were never yellow." Ten years before that he had composed a hilarious series of articles under the heading "Letters from a Badly Made Son to His Father in England," reporting on a mythical remittance man. Edwards' character was called Buzzard-Cholomondely, and in one letter he reported to his father that he has been shooting craps, which he says is "a different species of game from grouse or partridge." He then says he tried farming but soon lost a thousand pounds with the help of his "dear friends" Walker, Seagram, Dewar, and Gordon.[2]

The higher up in the social tree the English immigrants were, the less snobbish some of them seemed to be. Basil Aylmer, who eventually might have called himself Lord Aylmer after the death of his older brothers, was one of the most popular pursers on the Kootenay Lake ferry. Lady Aberdeen, the wife of Lord Aberdeen, who "showed the Scotch" more than he did and was certainly not a remittance woman, was in the Victorian Order of Nursing before she was married. She worked ceaselessly to offset the English class system. She was quite successful, as confirmed by a contemporary who said that thanks to her influence, "Vernon was a very friendly place."[3]

Aside from the results of primogeniture, mature male emigration from Britain to British Columbia started in the colonial days, with the arrival of British Army officers laid off at half pay following the Napoleonic wars, and continued into provincial times with Indian Army officers retiring on inadequate pensions. Both of these groups found that they could enjoy a higher standard of living in the colonies than in the motherland, and in western Canada they congregated around Calgary and the Alberta foothills, Vernon and the Okanagan Valley, Victoria and the Gulf Islands, Duncan, and the Cowichan Valley.[4]

The peculiarity of retired military men and remittance men was that many of them did not require any means of employment or sustenance. Their level of affluence varied, but some were extremely well-off with monthly receipts of as much as 300 pounds, more than a senior bank manager made in those days.[5] So when they surveyed their new locale from the sternwheeler and sought their own particular heaven on earth, they often looked for areas of scenic advantage rather than usefulness, a good description of much of the rugged coastline of Kootenay Lake and Slocan Lake to which many of them were drawn.

The difference between Okanagan Lake and Kootenay Lake, for example, was that alongside the latter, between the areas of relatively flat land inviting settlement there was usually solid rock, its front face often close to vertical. These beautifully scenic and idyllic, but otherwise rather impractical areas were easily reached at that time by the sternwheelers, which were plying the waters for the mining industry, and it was simplicity itself for the remittance men to take them up as the place to plant their overseas roots. The place names given by these British immigrants indicate their dreams. There was Destiny Bay on Kootenay Lake, Halcyon Hot Springs and Valhalla on Arrow and Slocan Lakes. (The Okanagan area was similarly rhapsodized with Kaleden, from the Greek word *kalos* meaning "beautiful Eden"; Sunnywold, meaning sunny open country; and of course Summerland and Peachland.)

Two sternwheelers on Lower Arrow Lake are surrounded by ice in 1890. Did they know at that time that compressed air bubbled slowly upwards would clear ice around a landing? This procedure is carried out today at Interior ferry docks. Obviously some clearing has been done around the vessel in the foreground.

The problems came when the sternwheelers departed the scene. The Department of Public Works' responsibility to build and maintain roads to many of these lakeshore settlements caused a big headache. The CPR's British immigration plan had caught the road authority again!

Before the remittance men arrived, however, the sternwheelers were already on the lakes and rivers of the area. While the introduction of sternwheelers to Okanagan Lake and to the Thompson watershed had been inspired by immigration and land settlement, the impetus for transportation on the Arrow Lakes, Slocan Lake, Kootenay Lake, Duncan Lake, and Trout Lake was mining and that alone. Between the years 1889 and 1892 five of the most productive lead, silver, and zinc mines that the world had ever seen came into being in the Kootenays and in the Slocan.

Ainsworth came into being in 1887, mostly because of the Blue Bell Mine across the lake but also because of its nearby hot springs. The town was further established when a namesake mine was built after ore was discovered in 1889. There was also a marvellous marble quarry in the vicinity, which supplied the Parliament Buildings in Victoria. Ainsworth was named for an American from San Francisco who acquired the site in 1883 and whose agent, Thomas Hammil, first claim-jumped at Riondel and then was murdered for it. Captain George J. Ainsworth became the promoter of the Columbia and Kootenay Railway and Navigation Company.

These mines, with the year of discovery, were the Silver King Mine at Nelson in 1887; the Ainsworth Mine in 1889; LeRoi at Rossland and the Payne Mine at Sandon in 1891; and the Sullivan Mine at Kimberley, the greatest of them all, in 1892.[6]

After the copper and silver find near Nelson, the next was a rich deposit of galena (silver, lead, and zinc) by Jim Brennan in 1889 above Ainsworth on Kootenay Lake. This assayed out as the richest silver ore found in the west, and Bill Barlee, in his television series *Gold Trails and Ghost Towns*, says that it yielded 1000 troy ounces to the avoirdupois ton. The developers of the Ainsworth Mine initially tried to "go Canadian" in co-operation with the CPR, and under the banner of the Columbia and Kootenay Railway and

The view is of Baker Street, the main thoroughfare of Nelson, the queen city of the Kootenays. Incorporated in 1897, it started off with its own water and electric power, which soon brought electric tramways. Nelson benefitted greatly from the fabulous Silver King Mine on nearby Toad Mountain, established ten years before, which led to the Hall Mines Smelter opening there in 1896. The city also obtained a more lasting bounty from the quick descent of the Kootenay River leaving the west arm of Kootenay Lake through a series of waterfalls, all of which have produced electric power and still do today. The main street is now a centre for the restoration of the fine buildings built in Nelson's heyday.

Navigation Co., William Van Horne built a 40-kilometre "portage railway" (a link between lake or river routes) from Nelson to Robson to transfer the ore from Kootenay Lake to the Arrow Lakes. This was followed by a long barge haul upstream to Revelstoke, where there was a smelter on the CPR mainline. This route proved unsuccessful because of the strength of the river's current, so the trip was too uncertain as well as too long. However it did encourage the CPR to build its line from Revelstoke to Arrowhead.[7]

The trigger for the CPR was of course the fast-moving enterprise of its stalwart adversary James J. Hill, who was invading Kaslo and Sandon to pick up the very rich ore from the Payne Mine, as mentioned in Chapter 5. The CPR was so anxious to get from

Sandon was staked out in 1892 after fabulous ore deposits were discovered by Jack Sandon in company with Eli Carpenter, whose name was affixed to the creek that ran through the middle of town. This creek, which was contained in a large, log-lined, box culvert under the main street, rampaged in 1955 and swept many of the ancient wooden buildings of Sandon into Slocan Lake, including the remains of most of its 24 hotels.

Nakusp, at the lower end of Upper Arrow Lake, became a major centre in the 1890s, rivalling in size its sister city Revelstoke, only a sternwheeler trip away. Revelstoke's rail line led to the rest of Canada, however, while Nakusp's went only to Sandon. The town suffered with the eclipse of the sternwheelers, but its scenic and wood-filled surroundings sustained it, as did its road connections when they finally came in.

Revelstoke to Sandon after completion of the line to Arrowhead in 1893 and 1894 that it could not wait for the ice to melt on Upper Arrow Lake in the spring of 1895. Construction crews dragged the railway machinery by sled over the ice to barges waiting in open water, and they completed their line to Sandon that year (see "Railways of Southern B.C."). This in turn led to open confrontation with the Great Northern railwaymen. The CPR built a station and freight shed on land in Sandon that the GN considered to be its own. When a judge upheld the CPR, the GN brought its men in from Kaslo and wrecked the buildings.[8]

As mining towns go, Sandon eventually went. It departed in style in 1955 when Carpenter Creek swept almost all of the old buildings clear out into Slocan Lake. (Nature habitually turned on these shantytowns. Tete Jaune Cache preceded Sandon in 1914; in that case down the Fraser. If it was not flood, then fire consumed them. This was the fate of Barkerville, Granite Creek, Fernie, and many more.) In the meantime, Nakusp, a town of substantial size and permanence, was established at the lower end of Upper Arrow Lake. There was no road at all to Nakusp. Other towns created in this mining frenzy were Rosebery, New Denver, and Slocan City; farther north were Argenta, Lardo, and Gerard, to mention the ones that stayed on the map. Slocan City was quite soon joined to the rest of British Columbia by a road, but the rest relied on rail or water for access for many years. This was no problem for the ore, but it was for the people. They soon wanted some competition to the CPR, as well as the freedom to move independently—the latter a necessity to their pioneering spirit. As well, the miners wanted access to the mines in all seasons.

But roads were not easy to build in that country, and once they were built they were difficult to maintain, especially in winter with the primitive equipment road crews had in these years. Between 1890 and 1915 over twenty lives were lost to avalanches in the Slocan, and a snowslide that came down off Reco Mountain into a narrow valley containing the road to Cody was so large that it covered the road to a depth of 170 feet and took six years to melt.

This is the valley of Carpenter Creek, which rises from its confluence with Slocan Lake near New Denver, B.C., within the Selkirk Range. It is a typical Selkirks "V-trench." The CPR followed this valley to Sandon. The downhill breaks in the timber cover in the foreground are the courses of mountain torrents, but the tree cover breaks in the background are signs of the mountainside logging that was largely responsible for the floods and erosion that destroyed Sandon in 1955.

The miners had to tunnel through it to get to the mine. (J.W. Peck, B.C.'s long-time, much-respected chief inspector of mines, included this story in a paper he gave to a conference on avalanche control. He also told how his car was trapped between slides near Sandon. He had to abandon it there and walk six miles out over numerous snowslides. He said that no one moved in the narrow high valleys of that area in the early spring after noon.)[9] These were all extremely steep valleys with high summits and heavy snowfall, conditions that slowed but did not prevent construction of the road that was finally pushed through beyond Kaslo.

This road continued south to Ainsworth and the mines there, but it went no further than that for many years because beyond Ainsworth lay the Coffee Creek bluffs, part of a 5000-foot-high mountain called the Balfour Knob. The slopes there were long and steep, and after a very heavy snowfall they were occasionally the scene of an odd phenomenon. When a cover of snow built up and started moving, it sometimes came down as a huge snowball that rolled along and left a strip of cleared hillside behind. This gave the same effect as when a child delightedly rolls a snowball across a lawn, but was rather distressing when viewed from the road below. The slopes were steep and unstable and a problem to the DPW for many years. The difficulty of building and maintaining a fully acceptable road to Balfour from Kaslo was one reason why the *Moyie* stayed in service for so long (see map "From Wagons to Motor Trucks" in Chapter 4).

Travellers had recognized the need for access to the Arrow Lakes from the Okanagan Valley as far back as the time of the Columbia River gold rush in 1865, when Colonel Charles Houghton blazed a trail over the Monashee Range to the mouth of Inonoaklin Creek on Lower Arrow Lake, a place later known as Edgewood. Houghton was a retired officer of the British Army and a veteran of the Crimean War. He arrived in the North Okanagan in 1863 along with Forbes Vernon and his brother, and became one of the first landowners in the area. He wanted a trail over the Monashees so he could ship his cattle up the Columbia River on the *Forty Nine* to the miners at Downie Creek. After the Columbia gold petered out, interest in the trail waned, with only a short revival during the railway construction in 1884. The railways and sternwheelers encouraged north-south movement for many years. It was the automobile and the need for an east-west route for cars that finally revived interest in the Okanagan to Arrow Lakes connection through the Monashees.

Local residents started agitating to have the trail converted to a road in 1914, and in 1916 parties of German prisoners of war started out from either end. Remoteness and other problems intervened, and after one season they were moved to Mara Lake. The prisoners finished five miles in rough fashion.[10] Years of inaction followed, and then another three miles were built by day labour in 1920. Work continued very slowly from 1922 to 1925, and a firm by name of Rawlings & LaBrash of Nakusp received four small contracts, one each year, to build another 20.5 miles and to renovate the prisoners' 5 miles. As this stretch neared completion, a primitive

The Moyie *at Proctor, B.C. The size of the steering wheel in the wheelhouse (six feet in diameter) is apparent in this photograph. As happened at least once, if the current caught the four large rudders and spun the wheel, and if the helmsman did not let go of the wheel immediately, he could be thrown through the side window of the wheelhouse.*

ferry service, made up of a launch and a raft, was installed, and on September 17, 1925, the 127-mile highway link from Vernon to Nakusp over the 4510-foot Monashee summit was complete.[11]

Public Works Minister Dr. W.H. Sutherland cut the ribbon on September 29, 1925. The opening had been delayed for two months after a forest fire destroyed two of the many timber bridges built for the road. It is not known whether Dr. Sutherland rode in the launch or on the raft across Lower Arrow Lake. He may well have stayed in Edgewood, where there was a splendid hotel. One of the contractors was struck by lightning that year, and it can only be hoped this was not from the wrath of God for unfair practices. The company was reorganised as L.H. Rawlings & Co., and it continued to win contracts—or be given them—building most of the road from Rosebery to Slocan City in the period from 1925 to 1930.[12]

In its annual report for 1926-27 the DPW published a map of the provincial road system as it existed in September 1925. This map shows the road to Edgewood, but no road to Needles and no ferry. There is a road shown from Fauquier to Nakusp, but nothing south to New Denver from Nakusp. New Denver is only linked to Three Forks, and Kaslo is joined to Ainsworth and to nowhere else. Howser is shown unconnected by road, and Beaton only to Trout Lake City. The gaps were labelled "routes proposed or uncompleted." There were many trails but a notable lack of roads, which of course was due to the presence of so many sternwheelers, though by that time they were entering their declining years.[13]

In 1931 a cable ferry went in from Needles to Fauquier. By that year the DPW had completed the Slocan Highway from Rosebery down to New Denver and farther south to Slocan City, a route along scenic Slocan Lake where the road varied in elevation from lake level to 1500 feet above it, either above or below steep cliffs. This connecting-up of roads coincided with the building of a road along Kootenay Lake from Kootenay Landing to Gray Creek, and the east-west linkage was completed when the *Nasookin* was chartered from the CPR as a ferry. It served until 1947 when a modern vessel went into service, running from Kootenay Bay to Balfour, a shorter trip than from Gray Creek.[14]

As well as this, the DPW purchased two more sternwheelers prior to 1930, both for the Ladner-Woodward's Landing route on the lower Fraser River, six miles from the Strait of Georgia. The *Helen W. Scanlon* was bought from a logging company and renamed the *W.H. Ladner*, and the *Beaver* (a successor to the original) was purchased from the CPR. The first mentioned also served on Pitt Lake.[15]

This was not the DPW's last experience with sternwheelers, however, as for a few weeks in 1951 the department chartered the *Moyie* as a substitute ferry, pushing a barge, while the new ferry, the MV *Anscomb*, took its first refit. The *Moyie* was laid to rest at Kaslo on April 27, 1957, and is now a popular tourist attraction.

By the end of the 1930s the days of the sternwheelers on Kootenay and Slocan Lakes and the lakes in between were over, and the road authority had mostly overcome the challenge posed by replacing them with roads. Most of the lakeshore communities created by the remittance men were finally linked by means other than water. A few decades would pass before Deer Park was joined to Robson on Lower Arrow Lake, and even more before Nakusp was linked by road to Arrowhead along the east shore of Upper Arrow Lake in the 1970s.

Why this section of road was not started sooner has never been clear. Possibly it was one link too many. Halfway along the stretch of lakeshore lay Halcyon Hot Springs and the St. Leon Hotel, the successor to a hotel and spa started there in 1889. This resort was very popular before the war, and it was an important stop for the sternwheelers. Visible across the lake were some of the highest peaks in the Monashee Mountains, and they made one of the most scenic views in western Canada. The property was purchased in 1924 by a man in the mould of the remittance men, a Brigadier-General Burnham, who put on full-dress uniform to salute the *Minto* on her last voyage to his landing on April 23, 1954. Sometime after that the large hotel burned to the ground, and General Burnham

THE SILENT WATCHMAN

When the Kootenay Lake ferry MV Anscomb *was hauled out of the water on the ways at Nelson in the spring of 1951 for refit and inspection, it was quite a problem to find a replacement for the seventeen days during which the vessel was out of service. This was one of the reasons why the operation was a year late in happening. Finally the CPR was persuaded to charter the last remaining sternwheeler on Kootenay Lake, the* Moyie, *to the Department of Public Works, along with a converted railway barge that the* Moyie *would push back and forth across the lake to provide the replacement car ferry.*

One thing the Canadian Pacific hierarchy would not contribute, however, for reasons best known to themselves, was a crew. Fortunately the chief engineer of the Anscomb *was a veteran of the sternwheeler days and held a steam ticket, so when he agreed to work a double shift that vital position was assured. All that was needed then was a captain, or better still, two of them. There were of course two captains on hand from the* Anscomb, *both mariners well experienced on coastal or deep sea service, but neither of them had experience with sternwheelers. They were destined to acquire that without delay.*

After a two-week shakedown period, during which the Anscomb *captains took the* Moyie *out in their off-duty periods, the most difficult manoeuvre was identified as the turnaround in Balfour narrows at the end of the trip from Kootenay Landing to Balfour. At this time of year the current was at its strongest, and turning a sternwheeler with a large steel barge attached to it in this narrow space with a lively current was no picnic. The senior captain studied the problem at length and drew up a written schedule, outlining step by step how it was to be done. They were ready to put the* Moyie *on the regular run.*

A surprise came to all on the first day of the charter period when a veteran captain of the CPR Lake Service entered the wheelhouse and took up station there. It turned out that a feature of the arrangement was for him to be there but to take no part in the operation at all, except to watch out for CPR property. His instructions seemed to include a requirement that he never speak. He became known as the silent watchman.

There was no engine room telegraph on the Moyie, *only a set of small bells called a "jingle" and a large ringing bell called a "gong" located in the engine room. These were attached to lines that went up through the ceiling of the engine room to the wheelhouse directly above.*

A signal from the bridge of two gongs and a jingle meant full ahead, two jingles and a gong indicated full astern, and so on. There was also a speaking tube, activated by whistling down it, which the engineer would answer if he heard it and if he had time.

On his first day out the second captain was returning to Balfour with a full load of what looked like very expensive cars. He was enthusiastically obeying the written procedure—following instructions such as "Wheel amidships, full astern," "Full left rudder, half ahead," in strict order—when he was diverted and suddenly realized that he had lost his place on the schedule.

The problem with the gong and jingle system was that when a signal was given there was no standing indication of the engine command in effect, and he could not recall what his last order had been. In other words he did not know whether the ship was going full ahead or full astern, and to compound his distress he had no idea where his rudder lay. All that he did know from looking out the window was that both the sternwheeler and its barge were in the grip of the current and heading for disaster.

This brings in the other problem, which was the steering system. It consisted of a very large diameter spoked wheel, located in the wheelhouse. To this was attached a drum, around which a stout manila hemp cable was wound three times, then led through rollers for the length of the ship to the tiller bar, which operated a large quadruple rudder. There was no reduction gear in this, the CPR disdaining such frills. When the rudder lay amidships, a white paint mark on the centre loop on the drum matched a marker. When it was not amidships, it was very difficult to know where the rudder lay, especially for a novice with the ship. As well as this, if the current suddenly swung the rudder, the wheel spun. If the helmsman clung too tightly to it at the wrong moment, he could be thrown through the side window—this had been known to happen.

In desperation the captain turned to the silent watchman and gasped pleadingly, "How's she driving?"

The watchman, with a look of total contempt, strolled over to the side window, glanced out, and announced, "She's going half ahead at full left rudder." With that knowledge the captain found his place, completed the manoeuvre, and docked the ferry.

The watchman's seemingly magical knowledge came from experience—when the Moyie was going ahead she yawed to starboard. The CPR never did make it easy for the road authority!

died with it. Was there a consensus that access to Halcyon and to the St. Leon should be only by water? And when the last means of that went did the old military man come to the sad conclusion that there was no point in carrying on? If so, then the ending for the hotel was as bizarre as that for the *Minto*. They simply torched the old vessel on the water in the middle of Upper Arrow Lake on a hot summer day in August 1968. After a full 70 years afloat on the Arrow Lakes, she burned beautifully. This was a true and fitting Viking funeral at the end of a period of adventurous over-the-water travelling in a different time and place.[16]

The Minto *was a sister ship to the* Moyie, *launched one month later than its twin in November 1898 at Nakusp. Its last trip was on April 24, 1954. This view is of the* Minto's *rather heroic demise by fire on its home waters of Upper Arrow Lake in August 1968.*

To be continued . . .

This story of the early development of transportation in British Columbia is completed in the author's second volume covering the central and northern parts of British Columbia— *Carving the Western Path, By River, Rail, and Road Through Central and Northern B.C.*

The Appendices

Appendix I, by an unknown B.C. government public relati(
officer, is one of the first press releases produced by the Departm
of Public Works. Written in 1911, it defends the choice of Gib:
Pass rather than Allison Pass as a way through the Cascades betw(
Hope and Princeton. It reads in places as if the road were bu
whereas it never was. Only 24 miles of roughed-out roadway w
produced on the Gibson Pass line before World War I. The r(
through Allison Pass came after the war.

Appendix II bears the signature of no less a person than Jos(
W. Trutch, later Sir Joseph. At the time he submitted this Min
to the Colonial Assembly, Trutch oversaw the Department of Lai
and Works and was Surveyor-General for the colony of Brit
Columbia. Assistant Surveyor-General Walter Moberly contribu
in great part, and the document is remarkably easy to read, des[
having been composed in 1868.

Why did the CPR later in the century not choose one or
other of the alternative routes laid out so comprehensively for th
in the Minute? Surely Trutch's masterpiece would have been availa
to them. At least they would have learned that Howse Pass \
lower than Kicking Horse Pass.

Howse Pass was obviously the easiest way through the Rock
and Canada would have had a much safer railway, if not quit(
scenic, from the beginning.

But politics and human nature intervened.

Appendix I

The Pacific Highway

COMMENCING at the international boundary of what was known as the Blaine-Vancouver Road [sic] but now is recognised as the Pacific Highway—the route travels in an absolutely straight line for some ten miles, having an excellent surface, giving the impression of an old Roman Road.

Tourists travelling on the Pacific Highway will naturally make a tour of Vancouver, crossing the Fraser River at New Westminster over the Provincial Government's Point Steele Bridge which stands today as a triumph of engineering skill, and a sign of the enterprise and faith of its builders. The Point Steele Bridge, which cost over One Million Dollars stands today—the route between New Westminster and Vancouver will shortly be entirely surfaced with a permanent pavement providing a drive way of exceptional quality between Sister Cities.

Proceeding eastwards the route follows along the old Yale Road constructed in the early days by the Royal Engineers, this road traverses the southern portion of the Fraser River Valley which is the centre of the farming industry, and, generally speaking, it may be said that there are few if any agricultural districts in the world of similar extent and fertility. The road is being rapidly widened out and improved to standard construction—an excellent drive may now be had to Chilliwack. It is hoped that with the completion of the Sumas Dyking Scheme all will be to the same high standard as from Chilliwack to Rosedale. From Rosedale to Hope reconstruction on the new survey has now commenced and though this work may take some time for completion, it will certainly be ready for the road through the Hope Mountains, when that is thrown open to Traffic and the road over Jones Hill, which for many years has been a menace to all kinds of traffic will be rendered innocuous.

Before the construction of the Canadian Pacific Railway a very careful examination of the stage route was made and it was determined at the time that the road could not again be thrown open to traffic without the expenditure of at least one hundred thousand dollars. With the construction of the Railway on the left bank of the Fraser River [the CNR]), nearly the entire old Yale Road has been obliterated. *(Ed.: This remarkable admission supports the belief that they never intended to replace the road in the Fraser Canyon.)*

It has been estimated that it would take the sum of one and a half million dollars now to construct a suitable road through the Fraser Canyon of suitable width and grade without interference with either of the Railways. As to the construction of a road directly from Yale to Lytton, one can only wait patiently to see what the future has in store. In the meantime a very excellent route has been located through the Hope Mountains during the summer of 1911 when the Public Works Department was fortunate in securing the services of Mr. A.E. Cleveland of Messrs. Cleveland & Cameron of Vancouver. Mr. Cleveland realises that the selection of the general route for the road was the most important consideration in connection with this undertaking and with this in view he made a very thorough examination of all possible highway routes south of the Fraser Canyon. Every known pass between the Coquihalla-Coldwater on the north to the Lightening Creek Pass [sic] near the international boundary together with all the routes leading to them were personally examined. Ultimately a location was made on which a road with grades not exceeding 8 per cent could be built at a reasonable cost, and it came as a matter of surprise to those who had a close acquaintance with the features of the broken country.

Beginning two miles to the west of Hope the chosen route lies by the way of Silver Creek, Skagit River, Cody Creek, Roche River and the Similkameen River. From the old Yale Road the new route winds pleasantly through stretches of the finest merchantable timber with every here and there a glimpse of the rushing Silver Creek, well named for its many cataracts. Further along the Kitsqua [Klesilkwa] and Skagit Rivers the road passes through beautiful areas of meadow land and alder flats, while in the valleys of the Roche and Similkameen, stretches of grazing land are passed through. Numerous mineral Claims are to be found located along the route and already the construction of the route has lent encouragement to the development of the mining industry. *(Ed.: Roche River is now identified solely as the headwaters of the Similkameen.)*

Apart from the attractiveness of the location along the rushing creeks and rivers and the splendid forested areas of the western section of the land, there exists within a couple of miles south of the Grand Pass one of the finest areas of mountain scenery to be found. *(Ed.: Grand Pass is thought to be Gibson Pass and this agrees with the elevation given.)*

The whole of the route is one of varied attractions for the Tourist and forms one of the most inviting sections of the Pacific Highway. The maximum summit is 4485 ft., but this will be reached with no greater grade than 8 1/2 per cent, the ruling grade being 8 per cent with only a short length of the maximum when this road is completed. The distance between Hope and Princeton will be about 95 miles, and doubtless before the opening of the road several stopping places or road houses will have been constructed along the road.

The present road between Princeton and Merritt, along the Tulameen River, presents many difficulties to travel—the section of the Southern portion of this route would in all probability have to be abandoned. *(Ed.: The reason was probably because the Great Northern Railway had crossed the Tulameen River three times in its construction, an excess designed to deny the Kettle Valley Railway access alongside it in the valley.)*

There is at the present time an excellent road from Princeton for several miles up One-Mile Creek and careful surveys for the continuation of this road through to Aspen Grove are presently being carried out. This will shorten the road between Princeton and Merritt by at least ten miles and though presenting considerable difficulties to construction, will eliminate a very dangerous section of road and will also provide a route through an unopen country and one which is not likely to be interfered with by the construction of Railroads as is the present road through Otter Flats.

From Aspen Grove into Merritt the road is rapidly being improved and brought to standard, all sharp curves being eliminated and the grade being reduced to a maximum of 8 per cent. The land to the north of Aspen Grove is presently causing considerable interest on account of the experiments in dry farming which are being carried out and have so far been so successful. The country around Merritt presents many and varied interests of an historical, commercial and scenic nature. From Merritt two routes are available to Ashcroft, one via Mamette and Happy Valley, and the other down the Nicola River to Spences Bridge and thence up the Thompson River to Ashcroft, the latter, however, presents many difficulties to improvement, and it is meantime the present purpose to ultimately improve the Mamette Road to Ashcroft—where the Cariboo Road is joined.

Leaving Ashcroft the Thompson River is crossed by a very beautiful wooden bridge which for the last two or three years freight traffic amounting to nearly one million pounds has passed. Several firms are presently engaged in the Express and Stage traffic on this road, some idea of the traffic may be gained when it is pointed out that during the month of October, 1912 one firm alone carried 118 passengers and over 16 thousand lbs. of Express freight.

Leaving the right bank of the Thompson River, the road climbs for a considerable distance then travels northerly on easy rolling grades to Clinton. The scenery on either end is of exceptional beauty and constantly changing in character. With a view to avoiding much of the freight traffic and dust a great deal of the automobile traffic is conducted at night, and one is to make the journey from Ashcroft to Quesnel in the still quietness of a summer's night to fully realise the beauties of the wonderful Panorama which is constantly unfolding, indeed one is torn between the desire to travel slowly and admire the scenery and the wish to open the throttle and take full advantage of the excellent surface with which this road is almost entirely provided. *(Ed.: This must be the only tourist promotion ever to extol the beauty of the landscape during the hours of darkness!)*

Between Ashcroft and Quesnel during the recent years the traffic on this road has been exceptionally heavy—this is duly accounted for by the construction of the Grand Trunk Pacific Railway, the prosperity of the mining industry, and the great influx of settlers who have been rushing in to locate and prepare their farms to be in readiness for the construction of the P.G.E. Railway. From Clinton to Fort George the Pacific Great Eastern will, in all probability, parallel the present Highway, but as has been found elsewhere it will be found that the construction of the railway will not diminish, but will increase traffic on the road and this will, apart from the fact that this road will form a section of the Pacific Highway, the Provincial Government are pressing forward the work in improving and surfacing the road as rapidly as time and money will permit.

Not only is the scenery along the road of a particularly pleasant nature, but if one has the time to take the journey by the stage, they will hear many tales of the early miners who attempted to carry in their supplies on the backs of camels and other strange animals, indeed even today bands of wild horses are to be found roaming the country—horses whose ancestors deserted the early miner during his rush to the Gold Field. One will also hear tales such as how four men for the sum of $100 carried a Grand Piano on their backs from Quesnel to Barkerville, a distance of 57 miles.

If they travel in the cool of the evening they will doubtless be rewarded a bear or a coyote cross the road and they will, at least, hear Coyotes howling from a very unpleasantly short distance. The traffic during the winter, has in the last few years increased so tremendously that special steps had to be taken to provide a suitable road, where, it was ultimately found that by the constant rolling of the snow, a hard pavement could be formed capable of carrying even automobiles or traffic and it is proposed in the future that the rolling will be continued as far as possible, so that the snow may cause as little hardship as possible. *(Ed.: For one who has maintained roads through Cariboo winters, the idea of a rolled-snow surface brings a shudder.)*

The distance from Ashcroft to Quesnel is 221 miles and all along the road at convenient distances can be found comfortable and commodious road houses whose Proprietors are willing to make a traveller's short stay as pleasant as possible.

Author Unknown.

(Oval date-stamped "Victoria Engineering District, July 11, 1913")

Final Note on the Pacific Highway.

This provincial government document admits "before the construction of the Canadian Pacific Railway a very careful examination of the stage route [from Yale to Ashcroft] was made, and it was determined at the time that the road could not again be thrown open to traffic without the expenditure of at least one hundred thousand dollars." The inference is that such was not forthcoming. It further states that the CNR had obliterated the rest of the Old Yale Road, and it would take a half million dollars to restore the route. This admission was the first by either government that there may never have been any intention to restore the road, despite the clause in the CPR contract requiring it to "keep all public and private roads in such condition as to be safe and convenient to the public," reported by the Assistant Public Works Engineer in 1922, after an examination of all the records. (See Chapter 2.)

This unsigned document has no official status—likely the reason there is no signature.

Appendix II

Introduction

This document is the most prominent statement ever made by the British Columbia colonial government on overland transportation. This Minute to the Colonial Assembly in New Westminster, submitted on February 10, 1868, by Joseph W. Trutch, was a blueprint for linking the colony with the new nation of Canada. It was necessary that any overland link be totally above the 49th parallel, the arbitrary boundary set by treaty between Britain and the United States of America. At that time, expansionists in a post-Civil War United States cried "54-40 or fight," so there was some doubt that the U.S. would continue to observe the boundary line.

There is no record of the Assembly's acting in any way in response to this Minute. Of course within three years British Columbia's citizens had agreed to become a part of Canada, lured by the promise of a transcontinental railway that would render superfluous the proposed coach road.

If nothing else, Trutch's document proves that had the railway not come to pass, British Columbia stood ready to do all it could to create a transcontinental transportation corridor outside, and fairly well removed from, the territory of the United States, which was far from a comforting presence at that time in history. Considering the resources available to those who prepared it—and Walter Moberly must be mentioned—it is a remarkable document for its scope and content.

Editorial comment is by the author.

An Overland Coach Road

MINUTE of the Chief Commissioner of Lands and Works on the subject of an Overland Coach Road through British Territory, between the Pacific Coast and Canada, comparing the merits of the various passes through the Rocky Mountains, and showing the extent of the road already built in British Columbia, and what remains to be done to complete it to the head of steamboat navigation on the Saskatchewan.

Little has hitherto been done towards the construction of trails or roads across the Rocky Mountains north of the 49th Parallel.

The primitive paths through the various passes of this Mountain Range, originally tracked out by Indians and only kept open year by year by their travel along them are still the sole means of communication between British Columbia and the North West Territory.

Some little work was indeed done, years ago, by the Hudson's Bay Company in opening trails through the Leather (Yellowhead) and Athabaska Passes, to facilitate the passage of their brigades, which at times carried supplies from the depots east of the Rocky Mountains to Jasper's House, and thence westwards, by the Tete Jaune Cache and by the Fraser River to the various posts in the region of the country now included in British Columbia; or southward by the Athabaska Pass, to the Boat Encampment and down the Columbia to the posts in Washington and Oregon. But soon after the Company established posts at Fort Vancouver and Victoria, supplied by ships direct from England, communication by these passes was discontinued, and the trails lapsed into disuse and were soon in no better condition than before they were improved by the Hudson's Bay Company employees. At present, except when travelled over by occasional parties of prospectors, or scientific explorers, these, as well as all other Rocky Mountain passes in British Territory, are made use of by Indians only.

Many of these passes are, however, even in their primitive condition, so easy of passage that horses carry heavy loads over

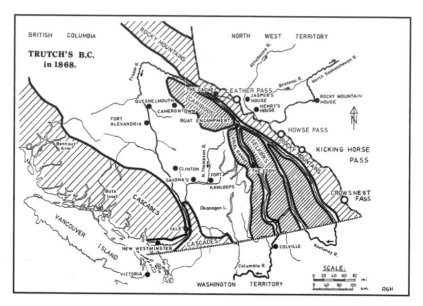

B.C.'s Mountain Ranges in 1868

them with facility, and through the Vermillion Pass loaded carts have been driven on the natural roadway unimproved by labour.

But, although the work of building a road over the Rocky Mountains has yet to be commenced, much has already been effected by this Colony towards the consummation of the much desired line of communication through British Territory, between the sea coast of British Columbia and Canada. In fact, more than one half (in cost) of this work within the limits of the Colony is now complete.

The Cascade Range of Mountains, the great barrier between the Sea Coast of this Colony and its interior districts, which presented a far more difficult engineering obstacle to road-making, and one more expensive to overcome, than the Rocky Mountains themselves, has been pierced by two lines of coach road, which, commencing at Yale and Douglas respectively, the limits of steamboat navigation on the lower Fraser and its tributary Harrison Lake, unite at Clinton, 136 miles from Yale on the high rolling plateau of the interior of the Colony, from which junction point the road extends 242 miles further northward to Camerontown, in the heart of the Cariboo District, distant altogether 368 miles from Yale.

A branch road, 23 miles long, has been built from the main line; from a point on the Buonoparte River, 110 miles from Yale, to Savona's at the lower (western) end of Kamloops Lake, from which place uninterrupted steamboat navigation extends through Kamloops Lake, and up the South Thompson River to the upper (eastern) end of Shuswap Lake, a distance of 115 miles, and also up the north branch of the Thompson River, which joins the South Thompson at Fort Kamloops, a distance of 85 miles from the latter post.

These roads, constructed at a total cost of $1,339,915, (about 275,000 pounds), of which amount the section from Yale to Savona's cost $830,000 (about 166,000 pounds), are of a character very superior to that of public roads in most young countries. They are 18 feet wide, the surface being covered with broken stone, where (as in most parts along the Fraser and Thompson Rivers) such material is at hand, or with gravel well cambered up in the centre, with ditches on one or both sides where desired.

With the exception of some short pitches as steep as one foot in ten, the sharpest inclines throughout this road are one foot in twelve, the curves being easy, and the bridges and culverts substantially built of timber.

Loads of seven and eight tons are hauled along them by mules or oxen at an average draught load of 1200 lbs. or 1300 lbs. to each team animal; and the Mail Coach drawn by six horses travels between Yale and Cariboo at a rate of nine miles an hour.

From the Cariboo terminus of this road, and from Savona's, as well as from the intermediate points along the road, various routes may be traced to the different passes of the Rocky Mountains. But before a judicious selection of the line for a waggon road to the territory east of the Rocky Mountains is made, it will be necessary to determine by more exact and detailed engineering explorations and surveys than have yet been made, which of these passes presents the least obstacles to the construction and maintenance of a road through it (with) as well the greatest advantages in its approaches, not only as regards engineering facilities, but with respect also to the character of the country to be passed through on either side of the mountains, its soil, climate, freedom from inroads of hostile Indians, and general capabilities for settlement, and especially in relation to its accessibility from the existing lines of communication in this Colony and to the eastward.

The following remarks embody the most reliable information extant on this subject; and the accompanying opinions and estimates based thereon are advanced in anticipation of the results of such a detailed survey which has just been suggested.

The passes through the Rocky Mountains at present known from the reports of various explorers, connecting with the Leather Pass, the most northerly point from which it would be practicable for a road connecting the Fraser River Valley with the navigable waters of the Saskatchewan to cross this range, and enumerating thence southward to the 49th. Parallel, are as follows, with their respective altitudes as far as they have been reliably determined by actual observation.

Of those the Athabaska Pass, although otherwise very favourably situated, is so elevated, steep and rugged as to be quite

		Altitude (feet)	Today's figure
1.	Leather Pass	3760	(3711)
2.	Athabaska	7000	(6512)
3.	Howse's	4500	(5010)
4.	Kicking Horse	5210	(5339)
5.	Vermillion	4903	(5416)
6.	Kananaskis	5700	(6444)
7.	Crow's Nest		
8.	Kootenay	6300	(Location
9.	Boundary	6030	indefinite)

impracticable for a coach road. The six last enumerated passes, although generally easy of passage, and in other respects available for road communication, are too far south for the purpose of such a line of connection between the sea-coast of British Columbia and the Canadas as is now under consideration, it having been determined by actual survey that no practical route exists for a road through the three parallel ranges of mountains lying between the Lower Fraser Valley and the Rocky Mountains, viz.; the Cascades immediately east of the Fraser; the Gold Range west of the Columbia; and the Selkirk Range in the Big Bend of the Columbia, and between that river and the Kootenay River, except that on which the road is now built from Yale up the Fraser and Thompson Valleys to Savona's; thence by Kamloops through the Eagle Pass, at the upper end of Great Shuswap Lake, to the Columbia River at the Great Eddy below the Little Dalles, and northward along the valley of that river by the Boat Encampment, and round the Big Bend southward past the mouth of Howse's Pass, of which line a more detailed description will be given further on, in connection with the Howse's Pass route.

The position of these southern passes is therefore, as regards their accessibility from the west coast very disadvantageous when compared with that of Howse's Pass. But they are still more ineligibily placed in respect to the approaches to them from the eastward; for these passes all debouch from the east into valleys, the waters of which are tributary to the South Saskatchewan, passing through a region of country beset with predatory Indians, and sterile and unattractive in comparison with the rich belt of land further north, through which the North Saskatchewan flows. *(Ed.: This paragraph is fully in line with the findings of the Palliser Expedition, members of which gave Trutch and Moberly a preview of their report. The work of Captain John Palliser and James Hector was highly praised by the colonial officials, and Hector's descriptions of the various passes, their nature, and their elevation were obviously used in preparing the Minute, despite it being published prior to the publication of the expedition report. Palliser stated that no suitable passes existed through the southern mountains west of the Rockies, and Trutch seems to have taken this as gospel, despite the existence of the Dewdney Trail. Trutch's Overland Coach Road stays well north of the South Saskatchewan River. He obviously believed the description of the Palliser Triangle, an observance which Rogers and Van Horne would have been wise to recognize fifteen years later. Strangely, Hector missed the lowest of the southern passes, Crowsnest, at 4534 feet, but it remains unlikely that Trutch or Moberly would have considered going through the desert-like triangle. Also, one of their major desires was to put the Cariboo Road, and its tolls, into the picture.)*

Through this rich district along the Saskatchewan, a line of communication between British Columbia and the Red River Settlement must pass, by whatever route it may cross the great watershed of the continent: indeed it may safely be taken as an established fact that such a line of communication must intersect the North Saskatchewan at Fort Edmonton, or some point higher upstream, so as to take advantage to the utmost the long extent of navigable water of that river.

From such point, however, the southern passes are entirely cut off. They may therefore be dismissed from further consideration in relation to an overland route through British Territory, the choice of which is thus narrowed down, as to the point of crossing the Rocky Mountains, to an alternative between Leather Pass and Howse Pass.

Leather Pass Route: The summit of the Leather Pass is the least elevated of all the known passes of the Rocky Mountains north of the 49th. Parallel, being only, according to Dr. Rae, 3760 feet above the sea. From Tete Jaune Cache at the western end of this pass on the Fraser River, in Latitude 58 degrees, 48 minutes north, Longitude, (about), 119 degrees, 50 minutes, to Henry's House due east, the distance is about 95 miles, the watershed being situated 25 miles west of Henry's House.

From Henry's House the pass turns nearly due north and follows this course along the Athabaska River 25 miles to Jasper's House at the eastern outlet of the pass. The total outlet of this pass is thus about 120 miles, in which distance no great obstacle to the construction of a road are presented by the natural formation of the ground, the chief difficulties being the swampy nature of the soil in places, and the frequent crossings of the mountain streams.

From Jasper's House to Fort Edmonton, the distance by the present line of travel is about 250 miles, through a rolling country gradually descending to the East but in great part swampy, very deficient in grass or other feed for stock, and offering but little inducement for settlement. The distance from Jasper's House to the navigable waters of the North Saskatchewan may, however be reduced to about 160 miles, by adopting a line intersecting that river at the junction with it of the Brazeau River. This line would pass through a country materially the same as that between Jasper's House and Edmonton, and on which the chief road making difficulties would be the great extent of swamps to be passed through.

The whole distance from Tete Jaune Cache to steamboat navigation on the Saskatchewan thus appears to be 280 miles, and the cost of constructing this length of road of the character of those above described and already built in this Colony, may be approximately estimated at $650,000.

From Tete Jaune Cache down the Fraser River is stated to be navigable for steamers with some three or four interruptions where falls and rapids occur, necessitating portages at these points, to Quesnelmouth, 320 miles from Yale, on the coach road between Yale and Camerontown.

The information obtained from persons who have travelled along this portion of the Fraser in canoes is too incomplete and wanting in detail to form the basis for any just estimate of its facilities for steamboat navigation; enough is known, however, to warrant the conclusion that the impediments to navigation will on practical investigation be found far more numerous and serious than they are now supposed to be by those who favour this line of route. At all events it is certain that this long line of water carriage, even if practical at any time, can be made available only for a short period during the summer and autumn; as the construction of a road along the Fraser from Quesnelmouth to Tete Jaune Cache is out of the question, not only on account of the distance between these points (330 miles), but especially because of the numerous steep and rugged bluffs which oppose the passage of a road along the banks of the river, it is evident that the Upper Fraser cannot be depended on as a permanent route of communication across the continent. *(Ed.: The problem of the rock bluffs is exaggerated.)*

The distance from Tete Jaune Cache to Camerontown, (nearly due west), the terminus of the coach road from Yale is not more than 80 miles as the crow flies, and it would therefore appear at first glance a matter of course that an overland route through the Leather Pass should be built by this route. But the intervening space is a sea of high mountains, so broken up into deep valleys and steep ridges that from personal information it seems impossible to connect the two points by a road of practicable curves and gradients, and we have therefore to seek in some other direction for a line of road between Tete Jaune Cache and the Lower Fraser. *(Ed.: This is borne out by Cliff Kopas in his book,* Packhorses to the Pacific, *wherein he describes a trip over Goat Pass via the Goat River, which leaves the Fraser 60 miles upstream of Tete Jaune Cache. Using this pass, Kopas crossed the Cariboo Range to Bowron Lake and on to Camerontown. Many goldseekers coming into B.C. by the Leather Pass went this way.)*

The most practicable route for such a road appears to be from a line running due south of "the Cache", across the upper waters of the Canoe River, (which falls into the Columbia at Boat Encampment), over the divide, (about 2800 feet above the sea level), between the stream and the North Thompson, and down the valley of the latter river to Fort Kamloops, to a junction with the present terminus of the coach road at Savona's.

The distance from Tete Jaune Cache by this route is 235 miles, the last 130 miles of which run through an open or lightly timbered bunch grass country along the banks of the North Thompson River and Kamloops Lake which are navigable for steamers throughout this distance, and on which waters in fact a substantial and powerful steamboat of 200 tons burden, built by the Hudson's Bay Company, is now plying.

The upper portion of this road between the Cache and the open country on the Lower Thompson, (a distance of 105 miles) would pass through a dense forest most of the way, but no high or steep summits have to be crossed, nor any serious engineering obstacles encountered.

The cost of a road between Tete Jaune Cache and Savona's may therefore be safely estimated at not more than $400,000.

There may exist routes (as some persons have stated) branching from the line just described, by way of the Wentworth or Clearwater tributaries of the Thompson, and intersecting the present coach road somewhere about Lake La Hache (210 miles from Yale). But the advantages which either of such deviations would offer in any respect over the route just described to Savona's are, to say the least, extremely doubtful, whilst on the other hand their disadvantages are obvious enough, of which it will be sufficient to specify one, namely: that, whilst these routes must cross over to Lake La Hache, through a district generally rough and timbered, and much intersected by swamps, the line to Savona's passes almost entirely through a near level prairie country.

In reference to this route from Tete Jaune Cache to Savona's, it should also be mentioned that besides the continuous navigation from Savona's extending thence 120 miles along the North Thompson as before described, there are stretches of navigable water of some fifty miles in extent on the upper portion of this river, which would be found of great avail both in the construction of the road and in assisting traffic along it.

It may therefore be assumed that should a road from the North West Territory cross the Rocky Mountains by the Leather Pass, it would follow this route down the Thompson to Savona's to reach the Lower Fraser: and taking Yale as the western, and the junction of the Brazeau River with the North Saskatchewan as the eastern terminus, the distance by this line, and the probable cost of constructing along it a coach road of a similar character to that already built in this Colony, may thus be recapitulated:

	Distance in miles	Navigable distance in miles	Cost $
Yale to Savona's	133	nil.	830,000 (already spent)
Savona's to The Cache	235	130 & 50	400,000
The Cache to Brazeau River	280	nil.	650,000
Total	648	180	$1,050,000

Of this line 305 miles remains to be built within the limits of this Colony, at an estimated cost of $610,000.

Howse Pass Route: Rocky Mountain House (3200 feet above the sea level), in Latitude 52 degrees 20 minutes north, Longitude 115 degrees 10 minutes west, and sixty miles upstream of the mouth of the Brazeau River, may be taken as virtually the eastern terminus of the route by Howse Pass, as from that point the Saskatchewan is navigable for stern wheel steamers of light draught throughout its entire course to the Great Rapids, 12 miles from its embouchure into Lake Winnipeg; and from there eastward the country is so open, and descends in so gradual and even plain to Fort Garry that a road may be led across it in any direction, with but little expense.

The line of this route would follow up the Saskatchewan to its source, and cross the watershed 145 miles from Rocky Mountain House, at an elevation of 4500 feet (740 feet higher than Leather Pass). In this distance the only material engineering difficulties occur in the last 20 miles, along parts of the road which would require to be protected from the force of mountain torrents, which at certain seasons inundated the river valley.

The crossing of the divide by this pass, in Latitude 51 degrees 00 minutes north, is stated by Dr. Hector to be very easy, indeed almost imperceptible, and he had but little difficulty in taking his loaded packhorses through to the Columbia, although no trail now exists through this pass, that formerly used by the North West Fur Company long since become overgrown and obliterated.

The descent towards the Columbia, although less gradual than the ascent on the eastern slope, is described as by no means precipitous or broken, but quite practicable for a road. The distance from the summit to the Columbia at the mouth of the Blaeberry River is about 30 miles, and the only obstructions noted by Dr. Hector in this section were the heavy forest trees and dense undergrowth and fallen timber which rendered the passage of his horses very tedious.

The entire distance from Rocky Mountain House to the Columbia is 175 miles, and the cost of constructing this section of road may be set down at $360,000. The distance from Blaeberry River down the Columbia to the Eddy, (in latitude 51 degrees, 00 minutes north, Longitude about 118 degrees, 00 minutes west), at the eastern end of the Eagle Pass through the Gold Range, which divides the Columbia Valley from Great Shuswap Lake, is 165 miles.

This section was carefully examined in 1866 by Mr. Moberly, Assistant Surveyor General of this Colony, with a special view to the construction of a coach road, and his report establishes the fact that such a road may be built without great expense along either bank of the Columbia; no extensive bluffs occur to oppose the passage of a road and at several points the river is so contracted that it may be spanned by a bridge of not more than 150 feet in length. The cost of such a road from Blaeberry River to the Eagle Pass has been estimated at $412,000.

Mr. Moberly reports however that this portion of the Columbia River did not at that season when he examined it (September) appear to him so available for steamboat navigation as had been supposed. The steamer Forty-Nine now plies between Colville in Washington

Territory and Death Rapids, 40 miles above the Eagle Pass; and above Death Rapids the river is again navigable to the neighbourhood of Boat Encampment, a distance of 40 miles or more.

But above this point there are several rapids which Mr. Moberly considered quite impassable by steamers, and which should therefore render continuous navigation below the mouth of the Blaeberry River impracticable.

The Eagle Pass was discovered in 1865 by Mr. Moberly, and has been subsequently surveyed by Government and a line of road marked through it.

Previous to Mr. Moberly's discovery of this pass it had been supposed that the Gold Range was a continuous chain of high mountains posing an insuperable barrier to any road between the Columbia and the Fraser River Valleys.

The summit of Eagle Pass, however, is only 280 feet above high water in the Columbia River, and 407 feet above the level of the Great Shuswap Lake, and the snow disappears from it in the beginning of April. From the Columbia River to the point where the Eagle River empties into Great Shuswap Lake is a distance of 37 miles, over which a road can be made for about $80,000. From this point there is, as before mentioned, uninterrupted steamboat navigation for 115 miles to Savona's, and steamboats may also run 6 or 8 miles up Eagle River.

To continue this route by land however to Savona's, the line of road would leave the Eagle River Valley at Three Valley Lake (20 miles from the Columbia), and run nearly due south through a wide grassy valley across a low divide to the headwaters of the Spillemacheene [sic] or Shuswap River which it would follow down past the mouth of Cherry Creek to a point about 70 miles from the Columbia. Thence leaving the Shuswap it would run through a district of open prairie and sparsely timbered land, abounding in rich pasturage, and along which are scattered several farming settlements, by a course west, 25 miles to the head of Okanagan Lake, and then 45 miles north-west to the South Thompson, and down

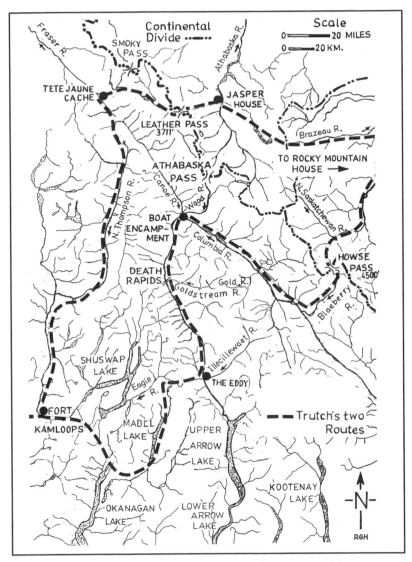

The Selkirks and the Rockies in 1868

the southern banks of that river and of Kamloops Lake, 40 miles through an open grass country, very easy to make a road over, to Savona's.

The distance by this route, and the estimated cost of constructing a road by it, are therefore as follows:

	Distance in miles	Navigable miles	Cost $
Yale to Savona's	133	None	830,000 Already done
Savona's to Eddy	180	110	240,000
The Eddy to Blaeberry R.	165	80	412,000
Blaeberry R. to Rocky Mtn. House	175	None	360,000
Total*	653	190	$1,012,000

* From Yale to Rocky Mtn. House.

Of this line 375 miles lie within the limits of this Colony, a road from which distance would cost $722,000.

It thus appears that there is very little difference in the distance by these two routes between the head of navigation on the lower Fraser and the navigable water on the North Saskatchewan, and that the expense of connecting these two points by road is materially the same by either route. The choice between them must therefore depend on more general considerations, in respect of which their rival merits can only be determined after more exact enquiry has been made, and as to which it would therefore be premature to hazard any conjecture at present. *(Ed.: Possibly, but the Eagle Pass route has it between the lines.)*

Although in the foregoing remarks the head of navigation on the lower Fraser has been treated as the western terminus of an overland route, there is nothing to prevent the line of road being continued, whenever the requirements of traffic call for its construction, from Yale down either bank of the river to New Westminster (a distance of 95 miles), which town is already connected by a road nine miles in length with Burrard Inlet, a harbour of great extent and ample depth of water, accessible at all times by vessels of the largest class.

It is only necessary to conclude these observations to refer to the routes through the Cascade Range from Bentinck Arm and Bute Inlet, by which it has been proposed to establish more direct communication between the Sea Coast and the Upper Fraser, in the neighbourhood of Alexandria and Quesnelmouth.

These lines have as yet been imperfectly surveyed and are therefore only partially known. It is however certain that the distance from Quesnelmouth to the Coast is less by any of these lines than by way of the Fraser River. There is also but little doubt that either line is practicable for a road although presenting obstacles to road-making, the difficulties and cost of which have been greatly underestimated, especially in the case of the Bute Inlet route. But when it is taken into consideration that the construction of this latter road from Bute Inlet to Quesnelmouth, a distance of 230 miles, is advocated as a competing line to the coach road already built it can hardly be believed that in the present state and prospect of business in this Colony such an undertaking can be seriously contemplated, nor is it reasonable to suppose that so unnecessary a section of new road from Quesnelmouth, running through tracts of land without a single white inhabitant, to a harbour of inferior character at the mouth of a narrow valley, affording hardly space for the site of a town, and but little land fit for cultivation, should, in place of the well established line to Yale be made part of a scheme connecting the Sea Coast of British Columbia with the Canadas, or that this latter most important object should be weighted down with the superfluous cost of its construction.

The various lines of route above referred are shown on the accompanying sketch map.

Joseph W. Trutch
10th. February, 1868.

(Note: As printed in the *British Colonist*, published in New Westminster on April 14, 1868.)

Final Note on Appendix II

Two routes that bypass the Fraser Canyon—that by Bentinck Arm, in the footsteps of Sir Alexander Mackenzie, and that by Bute Inlet, farther south—get short shrift from Trutch. The Bute Inlet route was a threat to the New Westminster interests that Trutch represented. It was strongly supported in Victoria under the leadership of Alfred Waddington.

Waddington's syndicate had sent surveyors to Bute Inlet and the Homathko River in 1861 and 1862, contesting the Fraser Canyon wagon road. In 1864, Chilcotin Indians massacred fourteen members of the survey party sent in that year. Waddington did not give up, even after the Cariboo Road became a reality. As the CPR surveys started he was in Ottawa, lobbying for the transcontinental railway to go by way of Bute Inlet, when he succumbed to smallpox.

A recently published letter (*British Columbia Report*, January 3, 1994) from John Waddington-Feather in England supports the position that Alfred was not a Chamber of Commerce man pushing his area, but rather a patriot, thoroughly convinced that the Americans intended to build a railway and occupy the Lower Mainland in B.C. Hence his efforts to secure a northern route to Vancouver Island. Early in the 1860s this was not the outlandish theory it gradually became. Waddington's mistake was that he did not give up on his obsession when it lost its validity—when the Americans had the rehabilitation of their southern states to focus on rather than looking north.

Chapter Notes

Introduction

1. Gilliland, "Arthur Kennedy's Administration of the Colony of Western Australia examined as a Background to the Initiation of the Vancouver Island Exploratory Expedition of 1864," *BCHQ* 18 (1954): pp. 103-115.
2. Harvey, *The Coast Connection*, p. 23; Palmer, *Report of a Journey of Survey*, p. 13.

Chapter One

1. Greene, *Personality Ships of B.C.*, pp. 19-26; Downs, *Paddlewheels on the Frontier*, vol. 1, p. 13.
2. Greene, *Personality Ships*, pp. 19-26; Downs, *Paddlewheels*, vol. 1, p. 13; Waite, *The Langley Story*, pp. 39-41.
3. Waite, *Langley*, pp. 38-39; Downs, *Paddlewheels*, vol. 1, pp. 21-23; Turner, *The Pacific Princesses*, pp. 2-3; Hacking, "Steamboat 'Round the Bend" *BCHQ* 8, no. 4 (1944): p.261.
4. Hutchinson, *The Fraser*, p. 154.
5. Large, *The Skeena, River of Destiny*, p. 115; Waite, *Langley*, p. 212.
6. Waite, *Langley*, pp. 157, 166; Downs, *Paddlewheels*, vol. 1, p. 42.
7. Turner, *Pacific Princesses*, p. 11; Greene, *Personality Ships*, pp. 43-47.
8. Downs, *Paddlewheels*, vol. 1, p. 26; Akrigg, *B.C. Chronicle: 1847-1871*, p. 218; Hacking, "Steamboating on the Fraser in the Sixties," *BCHQ* 10, no. 1 (1946): pp. 15-16.
9. Hacking, "Steamboating," pp 15-16; Hutchinson, *Fraser*, p. 158.

10. Some of the best descriptive writing on the Cariboo Road appears in G.P.V. and Helen Akrigg's *British Columbia Chronicle: 1847-1871*, which also includes a photographic insert. Material from old files of the Department of Lands and Works was used by H.L. Cairns of the Department of Public Works to assemble a great deal of information in his *Notes on the Road History of British Columbia*. More recent DPW file material from the 1920s, including a letter from James B. Leighton (DPW File 3464/23), was included in *The Coast Connection*, along with transcription of more of Cairns' information. Walter Moberley gives his version of the construction via Noel Robinson in *Blazing the Trail through the Rockies*.

11. Hill, *Sappers*, pp. 156-157.

12. Akrigg, *B.C. Chronicle: 1847-1871*, pp. 195-196; Hacking, "Steamboating," p. 23; *Cariboo Sentinel*, July 16, August 12, 1871.

13. Cairns, *Road History*, p. 19.

14. Chittenden, *Travels in B.C.*, pp. 25, 27; Turner, *Pacific Princesses*, pp. 6-7.

15. Downs, *Paddlewheels*, vol. 1, p. 33; Hacking, "B.C. Steamboat Days 1870-1883," *BCHQ* 11, no. 2 (1947): p. 103.

16. Waite, *Langley*, p. 114.

17. Harvey, *Coast Connection*, pp. 52-53, 57-58; Cairns, *Road History*, pp. 13-15.

18. Orchard, *Martin: The Story of a Young Fur Trader*, pp. 17-20.

19. Mackay, "Collins Overland Telegraph," *BCHQ* 10, no. 3 (1946): pp. 202-203.

Chapter Two

1. The March 11, 1997, issue of the *Victoria Times-Colonist* contained a report of the results of seabed drilling carried out in 1996 in Saanich Inlet. In the core sample was a paper-thin layer of muddy slime that was carbon-dated to 11,000 years old. The mud contained pollen that could not have come from the vegetation of the Saanich Peninsula. This pollen came from ancient hickory and walnut trees millions of years old that have

only been found in the Interior or Fraser Valley of British Columbia. The initial theory of the scientists was that the mud and pollen came to the Saanich Inlet from a huge and sudden outpouring of water from the valley of the Fraser, happening 11,000 years ago, probably caused by the melting and collapse of a glacier holding back a massive impoundment of meltwater.

2. Chittenden, *Travels*, pp. 38-42; Berton, *The Great Railway*, p. 210.

3. Chittenden, *Travels*, p. 41.

4. Berton, *Great Railway*, p. 210.

5. Berton, *The Last Spike*, pp. 185-187, 207.

6. Ramsey, *Ghost Towns of B.C.*, p. 188.

7. It is well recorded that William Lyon Mackenzie King, when he was a civil servant and deputy minister of Labour, came to Victoria in 1909 and inspected the opium factories, which were perfectly legal then. King drafted legislation to ban them. When it was passed the opium business went underground.

8. Berton *Great Railway*, p. 210.

9. Smith, *Widow Smith of Spence's Bridge*, pp. 39-41.

10. Berton, *Last Spike*, p. 310.

11. Smith, *Widow Smith*, pp. 26-27.

12. Green, *Above Stairs*, pp. 81-91 passim.

13. Ormsby, *British Columbia: A History*, p. 290.

14. Chittenden, *Travels in B.C.*, p. 41.

15. Ormsby, *British Columbia*, p. 296.

16. Harvey, *The Coast Connection*, pp. 59, 60; Cairns, *Road History*, p. 17; Atkins, *Columbia River Chronicles*, p. 102.

17. Robinson, *Building an Historic Railway*, p. 107.

18. Downs, *Paddlewheels*, pp. 8-9.

19. Smith, *Widow Smith*, pp. 39-40.

20. Atkins, *Columbia River*, p. 124. There was said to be a good business of rum-running to the "dry" railway camps. A few years later this route featured in the building of the Columbia & Kootenay Railway from Nelson to Robson, which opened in May 1891 to provide a rail and water route for ore from Ainsworth on Kootenay Lake to a smelter at Revelstoke. The adverse current on the trip from Robson to Revelstoke proved

insurmountable, and the smelter, which was running out of ore, closed down.

21. Atkins, *Columbia River*, pp. 124-125.
22. DPW File 3464 Special, 11/06/1880 - 12/11/1926.
23. Robinson, *Historic Railway*, p. 110.
24. Hill, *Sappers*, p. 128.
25. Robinson, *Historic Railway*, p. 105.
26. DPW File 3464 Special.
27. Ibid.
28. Ibid.
29. Ibid.
30. In his letter of June 30, 1876, to chief commissioner of Lands and Works Forbes Vernon, Road Superintendent George Landvoigt describes the 1876 flood. About the same date William Teague, the government agent at Yale, wrote to Vernon on behalf of Nick Black giving his report. (Harvey, *Coast Connection*, p. 58.) Teague states that the bridges at Anderson Creek, Four Mile Creek, and Eight Mile Creek simply floated away, and parts of the Quesnelle Bridge floated by. The water, he reports, was within four feet of the deck of the Alexandra Bridge. R.C. Harris writes that the damage to the Alexandra Bridge in 1894 was from debris hanging up on the under-the-deck wind bracing, not on the bridge itself, so the water level must have been very similar in height to that in 1876.
31. Robinson, *Historic Railway*, p. 105.
32. DPW File 3464-1 Cariboo Road, Yale District, 02/03/18 - 20/04/25.
33. DPW File 3464-1.
34. Ibid.
35. Ibid.

Chapter Three

1. William Mackenzie was always the financial genius of the pair, an aptitude he displayed even before linking up with Donald Mann, the master promoter. With some others he fulfilled the

compelling desire of central and eastern Canadian municipalities, especially Toronto, in the early 1880s for street railways. Using the proceeds from this along with Mackenzie's financial dexterity, throughout the following years the pair built up their rail network, culminating in the line through B.C. Their Canadian Northern Railway had a mileage of 1300 before entering the province, and they had just announced a general freight charge reduction of 15 percent, which was the reason Premier McBride asked them in. Their greatest good fortune was when the dominion government leased them all the lines the Northern Pacific had built into Canada, which the government had taken over as a result of public distrust of the Americans; their greatest triumph a three-mile tunnel under Mount Royal to bring their network into Montreal; and their greatest misfortune when, despite operating profits, their huge debt load brought them down.

2. Ormsby, *British Columbia*, p. 333.
3. Sanford, *McCulloch's Wonder*, pp. 139-141.
4. Ormsby, *British Columbia*, pp. 355-356.
5. Ibid.
6. DPW File 3464 Cariboo Road, Yale District.
7. Phillips, *Canada's Railways*, pp. 44-47.
8. Norcross, "The Coal Mine Tycoons," *Nanaimo Retrospective*, pp. 54-61; R. Stonebanks, "A Selfish Millionaire," *Victoria Times-Colonist*, May 4, 1997, p. E8.
9. Phillips, *Canada's Railways*, pp. 44-47.

Chapter Four

1. Chittenden, *Travels in B.C.*, pp. 50-63.
2. Ibid.
3. Cairns, *Road History*, pp. 20-21.
4. B.C. Archives and Records Service (BCARS), *Report of the Public Works Department for the Year 1902*; Cairns, *Road History*, p. 20.
5. BCARS, *Report for 1902*.
6. Ibid.
7. Ramsey, *Ghost Towns*, pp. 186-192.

8. BCARS, *Report for 1902.*
9. DPW File 5784-1 Kamloops-Cache Creek, 02/10-09/36; Harvey, *Coast Connection*, pp. 100-103. File 5784-1 contains an extract of a Road Bulletin issued by the Automobile Club of Southern California on June, 1 1927, which describes the road conditions as observed on a trip from Seattle to Banff, Alberta. The trip was probably made in the summer of 1926.
10. Downs, *Paddlewheels*, vol. 2, pp. 11-13.
11. Ibid.
12. DPW Files 3880-2 and 3880-3.
13. Harvey, *Coast Connection*, pp. 87-91, 94. Dr. James Horace King was the member for Cranbrook in John Oliver's Liberal administration in B.C., serving as minister of Public Works from 1916 to 1922. He handed over the portfolio to Dr. W.H. Sutherland, leading to B.C.'s duet of medical doctors in charge of roads. He later entered federal politics and served as minister of Health in William Lyon Mackenzie King's second Liberal administration, from September 1926 to August 1930. There is little doubt that he contributed greatly to the Big Bend Highway agreement, and it is unfortunate that he did not press successfully for the Rogers Pass alternative. During his time in the provincial cabinet he furthered the cause of roads in the Kootenay and upper Columbia areas, of course extending this to his time in Ottawa. By the 1930s this paid off with the route from Kingsgate to Radium and on to Banff. It became known as the honeymoon highway due to the number of American newlyweds who came up from the south by car to enjoy its good paved surface on their way to the Banff Springs Hotel. The road authority in B.C. certainly helped the CPR in this—but again, so did the dominion government!
14. DPW Annual Reports, 1924 through 1929; DPW File 3880 Roads Generally, Columbia-Revelstoke District.
15. DPW Files 3880-2 and 3880-3 Golden-Revelstoke Road, Columbia District, 24/09/28 - 30/12/39.
16. Unsigned notice entitled "18th Annual Slope Hazards Trip, Kicking Horse Pass, Field, British Columbia," *B.C. Professional Engineer* 47, no. 4 (1996): p. 17.

17. Alan Daniels, "CPR makes history again in Selkirks," *Vancouver Sun*, August 4, 1984, p. E1.
18. DPW Files 3880-2 and 3880-3.
19. DPW Annual Reports, 1933 through 1940.
20. The group consisted of Norman Zapf, assistant location engineer, Victoria, B.C.; A. Scarborough, location engineer, Nelson, B.C.; and J.P. Hague, senior location engineer, Victoria, B.C. Mr. Hague was subsequently seconded to the Canada Department of Transport, Trans-Canada Highway Division, in Ottawa, Ontario, as engineer in charge of the Trans-Canada Highway development in the western national parks.
21. J.P. Hague, "Selection of the Trans-Canada Highway Route Through the Selkirks," *The Engineering Journal*, June 1958, pp. 57-60. This is a transcript of an address by Hague, the senior location engineer for the B.C. Department of Highways. It was given to the 71st annual general and professional meeting of the Engineering Institute of Canada at Banff, Alberta, in June, 1957.
22. Alan Daniels, "CPR makes history again in Selkirks," *Vancouver Sun*, August 4, 1984, p. E1.

Chapter Five

1. Ormsby ed., *A Pioneer Gentlewoman*, p. xxvi. In these days, what they called the Similkameen in its last reach was what is now known as the Tulameen. Allison reported to Governor Douglas that he had found a south fork to the river, which initially was called Allison's fork, but which was later called the Roche River from the red mineral that led to Princeton's initial name of Vermilion Forks. Finally the Roche River became the Similkameen and the latter's north fork the Tulameen, both of which came together at Princeton.
2. DPW File 292 Hope-Princeton Road, 11/16-5/45; Harvey, *Coast Connection*, pp. 122-131.
3. Berton, *Last Spike*, p. 86.
4. Berton, *Last Spike*, p. 86, and *Great Railway*, pp. 156-158
5. Sanford, *McCulloch's Wonder*, pp. 27, 38, 39.
6. Ibid. 33-34.

7. Smyth, *Tales of the Kootenays*, pp. 76-77. The railway behaved very poorly when it demanded half of the townsite area of Fort Steele from the landowners, primarily the Galbraith brothers, especially as they wanted it without payment. The landowners refused. One of the Galbraiths ran the ferry over the Kootenay River and the other owned the general store. The CPR bypassed Fort Steele and established Cranbrook. Railway construction brought the East Kootenay area to life, including Fernie, Cranbrook, and Creston, and prosperity came with it, primarily from agriculture and coal. Many of these 5000 men who came to work on the railway were European immigrants brought over on CPR ships, and this is reflected by the number of residents of Scandinavian origin in the East Kootenays to this day.

8. Ibid. In comparison to the CPR's trouble with slopes in the clay and silt of this area, the slopes of Jim Hill's railway grade from Midway to Bridesville—excavated and compacted by the hands of the Chinese labourers—were as firm and unmoved in the 1970s, when they were examined by the author at the Harpur Ranch at Myncaster, as when they were first created.

9. Downs, *Paddlewheels*, pp. 44-54 passim; Riegger, *The Kettle Valley and Its Railway*, p. 82; Sanford, *McCulloch's Wonder*, p. 32. Hill's GN railway also acquired other railways in southern B.C., including the Nelson and Fort Sheppard Railway, which as its name infers ran from Fort Sheppard, across the border from Waneta, to Nelson. When it was built by American Daniel Corbin and approached its Canadian terminus in 1893, the CPR exerted its considerable influence on B.C. Premier John Robson and entry into the municipality was denied the railway. The American built his railway outside the city limits to the lakeshore at Five Mile Point, which was that distance east of town on the south shore of the West Arm of Kootenay Lake. Later, when the CPR acquired the Columbia and Kootenay Steam Navigation Company and competition finally disappeared, it refused to call at Five Mile Point—one more reason why Jim Hill had to build his own boats. The name of the point was eventually changed to Troup Point, after the CPR lake service's Captain Troup.

10. Sanford, *McCulloch's Wonder*, p. 43.
11. Harvey, *Coast Connection*, pp. 150-152; Sanford, *McCulloch's Wonder*, p. 44.
12. Sanford, *McCulloch's Wonder*, pp. 53-57, and *Steel Rails and Iron Men*, p. 9.
13. Ibid.
14. BCARS, Correspondence Outward (R.C. Moody), Colonial Files, April-December 1860.
15. Riegger, *Kettle Valley*, p. 194.
16. Sanford, *McCulloch's Wonder*, pp. 148-151.
17. Ibid., pp. 148-156
18. Ormsby, *British Columbia*, pp. 355-356.
19. Harvey, *Coast Connection*, p. 78.
20. DPW File 3464-1 The Pacific Highway, Cariboo Road, 5/11-4/ 26.
21. Harvey, *Coast Connection*, pp. 78-81.
22. Sanford, *McCulloch's Wonder*, p. 125.
23. Ibid., pp. 148-180 passim.
24. Riegger, *Kettle Valley*, pp. 151, 194-195.
25. *Encyclopaedia Britannica*, 1960 edition, s.v. "tunnel."
26. McCullough, *The Path Between the Seas*, p. 461.
27. *Encyclopaedia Britannica*, 1960 edition, s.v. " tunnel."
28. McCullough, *Path*, pp. 459-463, 532, 617.
29. Ibid., p. 503.
30. Ibid., pp. 539-550.
31. Ibid., p. 617.
32. Riegger, *Kettle Valley*, pp. 130-135.
33. Smyth, *Kootenays*, p. 89.
34. Sanford, *McCulloch's Wonder*, pp. 148-180.
35. Woolliams, *Cattle Ranch*, p. 16.
36. Ministry of Transportation and Highways, Hope-Merritt Highway Environmental and Geological Reports.
37. The map concurrent with the text at this point was based on one originating from aerial survey mapping carried out by the B.C. Ministry of Transportation and Highways for the design of the Coquihalla Highway and its avalanche protection program. The old KVR railbed was readily discernible.

38. Sanford, *McCulloch's Wonder*, p. 180.
39. Sanford, *McCulloch's Wonder*, p. 227, and *Steel Rails*, p. 94.
40. Sanford, *McCulloch's Wonder*, p. 242. The official's name was J.G. Sullivan.
41. Harvey, *Coast Connection*, pp. 29, 36-37.
42. Ibid., pp. 50-51.
43. This note refers to the map entitled "Two Routes from Hope to Similkameen." This map is taken from a plan found in Ministry of Transportation and Highways archives in Victoria. Both surveys are shown on Plan 1471, entitled "Hope-Princeton Road Survey Key Map." The scale is 1 inch to 1 1/2 miles. The map is dated April 2, 1924, and it is signed as approved on that date by W.K. Gwyer, district engineer in Penticton. An excellent reference for those interested in this terrain is the 1:50,000 map published in 1980 by the B.C. Department of the Environment entitled "Manning Park and Skagit Valley Recreational Areas," which is available at all bookstores handling government publications.

Chapter Six

1. Ormsby, *British Columbia*, p. 304.
2. Ibid., p. 314. Turner remained in the position until early in 1915 when Premier McBride announced an election, then delayed it, then resigned and advised the prime minister in Ottawa that he was appointing himself agent-general for B.C. in London, of course ousting Turner in the process. McBride had spent a lot of time in London since he was knighted in the New Year's honours of 1913, and he had watched the building of a new British Columbia House on Regent Street with great interest. His government went down to defeat in the ensuing election, delayed by the war. It is felt that he expected defeat and took the position in England to let himself down easy. McBride died on the day before he was to return to Canada in 1917. It must have been a disappointing dismissal for Turner, who had done well for the province.

3. Ibid., p. 353.
4. Mitchell and Duffy ed., *Bright Sunshine and a Brand New Country*, p. 11.
5. Mitchell and Duffy, *Bright Sunshine*, p. 25; Turner, *Sternwheelers and Steam Tugs*, pp. 21-22.
6. Akrigg, *1001 B.C. Place Names*, p. 106; Green, *Above Stairs*, p. 109; Ormsby, *Pioneer Gentlewoman*, p. 117n. Other members of the syndicate besides Lumby and Vernon included Francis Jones Barnard, the son of Frank Barnard, the legendary stagecoach owner on the Cariboo Road. Another was John Andrew Mara, for whom the lake was named, another well-known businessman, who not only was Barnard's brother-in-law but was also his partner in the Columbia and Kootenay Steam Navigation Company, along with Captain John Irving. That company was greatly interested in connections to the CPR mainline as it was very busy at that time hauling freight by water all over Kootenay and the Arrow lakes. However, even before the S&O track was laid, the CPR had an agreement to lease it. Whether the CPR told the S&O owners it was going to build its own sternwheeler on Lake Okanagan is not known, but by the start of 1897 the CPR had purchased both the S&O and the CKSN, and of course had the SS *Aberdeen* in operation out of Okanagan Landing. Long live monopoly! It was this process of elimination of competition that turned so many British Columbians against the company and caused them to support Jim Hill's defiance of it.
7. Mitchell and Duffy, *Bright Sunshine*, pp. 25-28.
8. Lord, *Alex Lord's British Columbia*, pp. 103-106.
9. Turner, *Sternwheelers*, p. 24; Mitchell and Duffy, *Bright Sunshine*, p. 15.
10. In the *British Columbia Chronicle: 1847-1871*, authors G.P.V. and Helen Akrigg relate the story of a goldseeker by name of Herman Francis Reinhart who was one of a party of Americans who came into the Okanagan Valley in 1858. The group split above the border and 100 left for the Fraser Valley, the others continuing northwards. Possibly as many as 300 strong, they behaved like invading troops with advance and flanking parties:

the native Indians were the enemy. An action took place resulting in ten or twelve Natives dead and two prisoners taken. When the Americans reached Fort Kamloops, their welcome was a thorough dressing-down by a courageous old Shuswap chief. American losses were not revealed, but when a number of French-Canadian voyageurs who were accompanying them left in disgust, one of the voyageurs fell behind and was killed. Many of the Americans were ashamed. They broke into smaller groups and moved to the Nicoamen Creek area after gold. The ones who went to the Fraser also attacked a group of Natives. This ill-advised foray had lasting repercussions on Canadian-American relations.

11. Mitchell and Duffy, *Bright Sunshine*, p. iv; Ormsby, *Pioneer Gentlewoman*, pp. 114n, 118n, 123n.

12. Mitchell and Duffy, *Bright Sunshine*, pp. 2-9.

13. Ibid.

14. Ibid., p. 24; Downs, *Paddlewheels*, vol 2., pp. 15-16.

15. Ormsby, *Pioneer Gentlewoman*, p. 117n; Harvey, *Coast Connection*. p. 60.

16. Harvey, *Coast Connection*, pp. 50-51, 66; Gould, *Ranching*, p. 143.

17. Mitchell and Duffy, *Bright Sunshine*, pp. 20, 54-73 passim. Robinson moved to Trout Creek and founded Summerland, and eventually to Naramata where he retired and where he died in 1932. He was a man of great stature. Another land developer from Manitoba was James Ritchie, who came in 1903 and who managed to exchange purchased land for an Indian reserve at Siwash Flats, which he converted into West Summerland. He developed Kaleden on Skaha Lake and there he built a multi-storied hotel out of concrete. Quite an innovation for B.C. in these years, it was at least more fireproof than the wooden hotels that regularly burned down. It disappeared with World War I.

18. Ibid., p. 19.

19. Ibid., p. 27-28.

20. Ibid., p. 73-74; Ormsby, *British Columbia*, pp. 375-377,

401-402.

21. DPW File 1643 Lakeshore Road, North & South Okanagan District.

22. DPW File 1643 and DPW Annual Report, 1929-30, p. T17.

23. Mitchell and Duffy, *Bright Sunshine*, p. 28.

24. Ibid., pp. 1, 37.

25. Dunae, *Gentlemen Emigrants*, pp. 221-222.

26. Harvey, *Coast Connection*, p. 211.

27. BCARS, *Report for 1902*; Cairns, *Road History*, p. 20.

28. Harvey, *Coast Connection*, pp. 20-27 passim; Akrigg, *B.C. Chronicle: 1778-1846*, p. 236.

29. DPW File 1643.

30. Turner, *Sternwheelers*, pp. 191-193.

31. Ibid. p. 206.

32. DPW File 1643 and DPW Annual Reports, 1934 through 1940.

33. Mitchell and Duffy, *Bright Sunshine*, pp. 23-24. Paddy Acland was so productive of historical commentary on events of the first decade of the twentieth century in the Okanagan Valley that around 1975 the Sound Heritage Program produced a special audiocassette program of his interviews, entitled *Paddy Acland's Progress: The Adventures of a Young Englishman in the Okanagan Valley*. The tape is available from the British Columbia Archives and Records Service.

Chapter Seven

1. Mitchell and Duffy, *Bright Sunshine*, pp. 19-48 passim; Dunae, *Gentlemen Emigrants*, pp. 2-8, 43-45, 123-227 passim. Both these volumes give good coverage of the remittance men. The first relates to British Columbia and the Okanagan and benefits from first-hand or son or daughter interviews. Old-timers Paddy Acland, Dorothea Wilson, Dorothy Robinson, R.J. Sugars, Bob Gammon, Tommy Wilmot, and others give insight into a wonderful society in the valley in the twenty years before World War I. In the second book, Patrick Dunae brings in all areas of Canada, as well as covering B.C. extensively.

2. Dunae, *Gentlemen Emigrants*, p. 139

3. Mitchell and Duffy, *Bright Sunshine*, pp. 40-41.
4. Dunae, *Gentlemen Emigrants*, pp. 1-12.
5. Mitchell and Duffy, *Bright Sunshine*, pp. 36-38.
6. Smyth, *Kootenays*, pp. 8, 13.
7. Bryan, *Backroads of British Columbia*, p. 136; Sanford, *McCulloch's Wonder*, pp. 20-21, 27-28.
8. Ibid.
9. Gold and Williams ed., *Ice Engineering and Avalanche Forecasting and Control*, p. 79.
10. DPW File 1752, Edgewood-Vernon Road.
11. B.R. Atkins, "Edgewood to Vernon Motor Road," *Vancouver Province*, September 20, 1925.
12. Ibid.; DPW Annual Reports, 1925 through 1930.
13. DPW Annual Reports, 1925 through 1930.
14. DPW Annual Report, 1931-32, p. M5; Clapp, *Lake and River Ferries*, pp. 32-47 passim.
15. Turner, *Sternwheelers*, p. 271.
16. Ibid., p. 228; Downs, *Paddlewheels*, vol. 2, pp. 57-58. The vessel's last fourteen years were anti-climactic. After being sold for junk it was rescued by a nostalgic farmer, but John Nelson could not afford to refit the boat for display, and when he died it followed him to the grave.

BIBLIOGRAPHY

Akrigg, G.V.P. and Helen B. *British Columbia Chronicle: 1778-1846*. (Vancouver: Discovery Press, 1975).
_____*British Columbia Chronicle: 1847-1871*. (Vancouver: Discovery Press, 1977).
_____*1001 British Columbia Place Names*. (Vancouver: Discovery Press, 1969).
Atkins, B.R. *Columbia River Chronicles*. (Vancouver: The Alexander Nicholls Press, 1976).
Baynes, Raymond. *Frontier to Freeway*. (Victoria: Ministry of Transportation & Highways, 1971).
Berton, Pierre. *The National Dream*. (Toronto: McClelland & Stewart, 1970)
_____*The Last Spike*. (Toronto: McClelland & Stewart, 1971).
_____*The Great Railway*. (Toronto: McClelland & Stewart, 1972).
B.C. Ministry of Transportation & Highways. "Hope-Merritt Highway. Corridor, Surficial Geology." 1978.
_____"Hope-Merritt Highway. Preliminary Environmental Report." 1978.
Bryan, Liz & Jack. *Backroads of British Columbia*. (Vancouver: Sunflower Books, 1975).
Cairns, H.L. *Notes on Road History of British Columbia*. (Victoria: DPW Archives).
Chittenden, Newton H. *Travels in British Columbia*. (Vancouver: Gordon Soules Book Publishers, 1984—original 1882).
Clapp, Frank A. *Lake and River Ferries*. (Victoria: DPW Archives, 1991).
Coutts, R. *Yukon Places and Names*. (Sidney, B.C.: Gray's Publishing Ltd., 1980).
Downs, Art. *Paddlewheels on the Frontier*. Volumes One & Two. (Surrey, B.C.: Foremost Publishing Ltd., 1971).
_____*Wagon Road North*. (Quesnel, B.C.: Northwest Digest Ltd., 1960/61).

Dunae, Patrick A. *Gentlemen Emigrants*. (Vancouver: Douglas & McIntyre, 1981).

Durnford, Hugh, ed. *Heritage of Canada*. (Montreal: The Canadian Automobile Association with the Reader's Digest Association (Canada) Ltd., 1978).

Farley, Albert L. *Atlas of British Columbia*. (Vancouver: UBC Press, 1979).

Fetherling, Douglas. *The Gold Crusades: A Social History of Gold Rushes, 1849-1929*. (Toronto: Macmillan of Canada, 1988).

Fraser, Colin. *The Avalanche Enigma*. (London: John Munroe, 1966).

Gilliland, H.C. "Arthur Kennedy's Administration of the Colony of Western Australia examined as a Background to the Initiation of the Vancouver Island Exploratory Expedition of 1864." *B.C. Historical Quarterly* 18 (1954).

Gold, L.W. and G.B. Williams, ed.. *Ice Engineering and Avalanche Forecasting and Control*. (Ottawa: The National Research Council, 1969).

Gould, Ed. *Ranching*. (Saanichton, B.C.: Hancock House Publishers Ltd., 1978).

Green, Valerie. *Above Stairs: Social Life in Upper Class Victoria 1843-1918*. (Victoria: Sono Nis Press, 1995).

Greene, Ruth. *Personality Ships of British Columbia*. (West Vancouver: Marine Tapestry Publications Ltd., 1969).

Hacking, Norm. *Captain William Moore*. (Surrey, B.C.: Heritage House Pub. Co. Ltd., 1993).

———"B.C. Steamboat Days 1870-1883." *B.C. Historical Quarterly* 11, no. 2 (April 1947).

———"Steamboat 'Round the Bend." *B.C. Historical Quarterly* 8, no. 4 (October 1944).

———"Steamboating on the Fraser in the Sixties." *B.C. Historical Quarterly* 10, no. 1 (January 1946).

Hague, J.P. "Selection of the Trans-Canada Highway Route through the Selkirk Mountains." *The Engineering Journal* (June 1958).

Hardy, W.G. *From Sea Unto Sea*. (Toronto: Popular Library, 1960).

Harris, R.C. "The First Alexandra Bridge: 1863-1912." *B.C. Historical News* (Fall 1982).

Harvey, R.G. *The Coast Connection*. (Lantzville, B.C.: Oolichan Books, 1994).

Hill, Beth. *Sappers: The Royal Engineers in British Columbia*. (Ganges, B.C.: Horsdal & Schubart, 1987).

Hutchinson, Bruce. *The Fraser*. Rivers of America Books. (New York/ Toronto: Rinehart and Co., 1950).

Johnston, Lukin. *Beyond the Rockies*. (London: J.M. Dent & Sons Ltd., 1929).

Kopas, Cliff. *Packhorses to the Pacific*. (Sidney, B.C.: Gray's Publishing Ltd., 1976).

Large, Dr. R.G. *The Skeena: River of Destiny*. (Vancouver: Mitchell Press and Victoria: Gray's Publishing Ltd., 1957).

Lord, Alex. *Alex Lord's British Columbia*. (Vancouver, B.C.: UBC Press, 1992).

Mackay, Corday. "Collins Overland Telegraph." *B.C. Historical Quarterly* 10, no. 3 (July 1946).

McCullough, David. *The Path Between the Seas: Creation of the Panama Canal. 1870-1914*. (New York: Simon & Schuster Inc., 1977).

Mitchell, David and Denis Duffy, eds. *Bright Sunshine and a Brand New Country: Recollections of the Okanagan Valley 1890-1914*. Sound Heritage Volume VIII No. 3. Aural History Program. (Victoria: B.C. Archives & Records Service, 1979).

Moody, Lt. Col. R.C. "Correspondence Outwards April-December, 1860." (Victoria: B.C. Archives & Records Service).

Norcross, E. Blanche, ed. *Nanaimo Retrospective: The First Century*. (Nanaimo, B.C.: Nanaimo Historical Society, 1979).

Orchard, Imbert, ed. *Martin: The Story of a Young Fur Trader*. Sound Heritage No. 30. Aural History Program. (Victoria: B.C. Archives & Records Service, 1981).

Ormsby, M. A. *British Columbia: A History*. (Toronto: Macmillan, 1958).

_____ed. *A Pioneer Gentlewoman in British Columbia: The Recollections of Susan Allison*. (Vancouver: UBC Press, 1976).

Palmer, Lt. R.C. *Report of a Journey of Survey, 1862*. (Victoria: B.C. Archives and Records Services).

Phillips, R.A.J. *Canada's Railways*. Canada at Work Series. (Toronto: McGraw-Hill Company of Canada Limited, 1968).

Ramsey, Bruce. *Ghost Towns of British Columbia*. (Vancouver: Mitchell Press Limited, 1963).

Reigger, Hal. *The Kettle Valley and Its Railway*. (Edmonds, WA: Pacific Fast Mail, 1981).

Robinson, Noel, and the Old Man Himself. *Blazing the Trail Through the Rockies: The Story of Walter Moberly* and *Building An Historic Railway: The Memoirs of H.J. Cambie*. (One volume). (New

Westminster: News Advertiser Printers and Bookbinders).

Sanford, Barrie. *McCulloch's Wonder: The Story of the Kettle Valley Railway.* (West Vancouver: Whitecap Books, 1979).

————*Steel Rails and Iron Men: A Pictorial History of the Kettle Valley Railway.* (West Vancouver: Whitecap Books, 1990).

Smith, Jessie Ann. *Widow Smith of Spence's Bridge.* Meryl J. Campbell and Audrey Ward, eds. (Merritt, B.C.: Sonotek Publishing, 1984).

Smyth, Fred. J. *Tales of the Kootenays.* (Vancouver: Douglas & McIntyre, 1938 and 1977).

Turner, Robert D. *The Pacific Princesses.* (Victoria: Sono Nis Press, 1977).

————*Sternwheelers and Steam Tugs.* (Victoria: Sono Nis Press, 1984).

Waite, Donald E. *The Langley Story.* (Langley, B.C.: Don Waite Publishing, 1977).

White, Howard, ed. *Raincoast Chronicles First Five.* (Madeira Park, B.C.: Harbour Publishing, 1976).

Woolliams, Nina G. *Cattle Ranch: The Story of the Douglas Lake Cattle Company.* (Vancouver: Douglas & McIntyre, 1979).

Video Presentations

Barlee, Bill and Mike Roberts. Television series entitled *Gold Trails and Ghost Towns.* Produced by station CHBC, Kelowna, B.C.

Newspapers and Other Publications

B.C. Department of Public Works/Department of Highways Annual Reports.

B.C. Professional Engineer. (Journal of the Association of Professional Engineers and Geoscientists of B.C.

British Columbia Report.

The British Colonist. (New Westminster. 1868, 1869)

The Cariboo Sentinel.

The Vancouver Province.

The Vancouver Sun.

The Victoria Times-Colonist.

Index

Photo Credits

BC Archives: A-1230 (p. 10), A-00011 (p. 20), D-00389 (p. 22, br), D-05578 (p. 26), A-05705 (p. 27), A-3876 (p. 28), A-1990 (p. 34), A-03951 (p. 35), A-03868 (p. 40, t), F-09265 (p. 40, bl), D-06672 (p. 40, br), I-30869 (p. 43), A-03928 (p. 47), F-08418 (p. 51), 2101 (p. 52, tl), G-02166 (p. 52, tr), A-1814 (p. 52, bl), H-00791 (p. 52, br), B-667 (p. 54), A-00107 (p. 56), C-08525 (p.57), D-08785 (p. 58), A-09251 (p. 59), A-01836 (p. 61), B-06922 (p. 67, l), B-06923 (p. 67, r), G-08302 (p. 69), PDP-02261 (p. 70), D-05673 (p. 72, l), B-09844, (p. 72, m), A-2489 (p. 72, r), A-3631 (p. 80), A-00873 (p. 82), D-00047 (p. 85), F-00333 (p. 87), D-02736 (p. 90), B-08415 (p. 93), D-183 (p. 94 i), E-332 (p. 94, t), D-182 (p. 96, m), F-6223 (p. 96, b), A-9833 (p. 97, br), D-02816 (p. 101), I-51739 (p. 102), D-8228 (p. 108, t), A-1961 (p. 108, i), B-00880 (p. 109, r), B-06638 (p: 109, tl), C-8567 (p. 118, l), A-3533 (p. 118, r), A-8880 (p. 138, t), c-8276 (p. 138, b), F-04508 (p. 144), PDP 01174 (p. 152, m), B-09611 (p. 152, b), G-08301 (p. 153), A-06249 (p. 165, t), F-02742 (p. 165, b), A-00143 (p. 167), D-1754 (p. 173), (p. 174), A-00321 (p. 179); Canadian Pacific Corporate Archives: 3068 (p. 97 bl) 25994 (p. 97 tr), Dept. of Travel Industry, B.C. Gov't.: (p. 129); Engler, B.: (p. 91); Glacier National Park, John G. Woods: (p. 106 tr); Glenbow Alberta Institute: NA 2115-2 (p. 97 tl) (p. 132); Harvey, R.G.: (p. 140); Heritage House collection: (p. 22 t, bl, bm, 24, 32, 33, 83, 84, 111 b, front cover and p. 115, 125, 152 t, 154, 157, 168, 172, 175, 184); Miller, A.: (p. 22 bl), Public Archives of Canada: 25036 (p. 44); Tourism B.C.: 13359N (p. 106 tl), 4118N (p. 106 b), 07-00494 (p. 177); VPL: 3263 (p. 42), 723(p. 96t)
(Code: t-top, b-bottom, l-left, r-right, m-middle, i-insert)

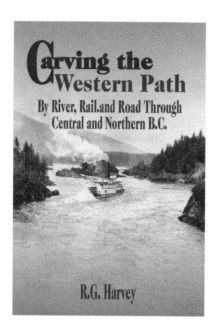

Carving the Western Path: By River, Rail, and Road Through Central and Northern B.C., the companion to this book, is also published by Heritage House. ISBN 1-895811-74-0

The Author

Bob Harvey joined the Department of Public Works of British Columbia in May of 1948, right in the middle of the worst spring flooding in 54 years. After some years as District Engineer at Nelson, then a few as the same at Nanaimo, he became Regional Maintenance Engineer at New Westminster, responsible for all provincial roads in Skeena, Prince Rupert, and Atlin districts, as well as Vancouver Island and the Lower Mainland. In 1958 he became Regional Highway Engineer at Prince George, in what was by then the Ministry of Highways, taking the northern districts with him to become responsible for all provincial roads north of Williams Lake. He moved to Victoria in 1967 and became Deputy Minister of Highways and Public Works in 1976. He retired in 1983.